Physical Characteristics
of the Greyhound

(from the American Kennel Club breed standard)

Back: Muscular and broad.

Loins: Good depth of muscle, well arched, well cut up in the flanks.

Tail: Long, fine and tapering with a slight upward curve.

Hindquarters: Long, very muscular and powerful, wide and well let down, well-bent stifles. Hocks well bent and rather close to ground, wide but straight fore and aft.

Weight: Dogs, 65 to 70 pounds; bitches 60 to 65 pounds.

Feet: Hard and close, rather more hare than catfeet, well knuckled up with good strong claws.

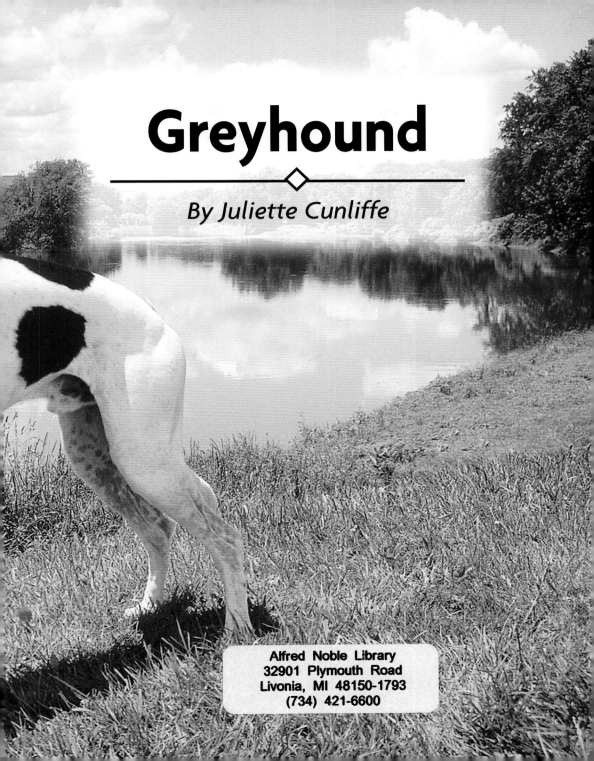

Greyhound

◇

By Juliette Cunliffe

9

History of the Greyhound

Follow the breed's long and varied history—from its ancient beginnings as a venerated sight hound, to valued hunter of British royalty, to competitive courser and racer, to increasingly popular companion and show dog known to fanciers the world over.

26

Characteristics of the Greyhound

The sleek, graceful lines of an athlete paired with the heart of a champion, the Greyhound is much more than just a racing dog. Meet the gentle, expressive and intelligent personality behind the physical beauty and learn why a growing number of people are choosing to share their lives with this wonderful breed.

36

Breed Standard for the Greyhound

Learn the requirements of a well-bred Greyhound by studying the description of the breed set forth in the American Kennel Club standard. Both show dogs and pets must possess key characteristics as outlined in the breed standard.

42

Your Puppy Greyhound

Be advised about choosing a reputable breeder and selecting a healthy, typical puppy. Understand the responsibilities of ownership, including home preparation, acclimatization, the vet and prevention of common puppy problems.

68

Everyday Care of Your Greyhound

Enter into a sensible discussion of dietary and feeding considerations, exercise, grooming, traveling and identification of your dog. This chapter discusses Greyhound care for all stages of development.

82

Training Your Greyhound

By Charlotte Schwartz
Be informed about the importance of training your Greyhound from the basics of house-training and understanding the development of a young dog to executing obedience commands (sit, stay, down, etc.).

Contents

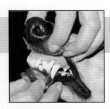

KENNEL CLUB BOOKS: GREYHOUND
ISBN: 978-1-59378-237-5

Copyright © 2004, **2008** • Kennel Club Books® • A Division of BowTie, Inc.
40 Main Street, Freehold, NJ 07728 USA
Cover Design Patented: US 6,435,559 B2 • Printed in South Korea

Photography by Carol Ann Johnson
with additional photographs by

Norvia Behling, T. J. Calhoun, Carolina Biological Supply, Juliette Cunliffe, Doskocil, Isabelle Français, James Hayden-Yoav, James R. Hayden, RBP, Bill Jonas, Dwight R. Kuhn, Dr. Dennis Kunkel, Mikki Pet Products, Phototake, Jean Claude Revy, Steve Sourifman, Dr. Andrew Spielman and C. James Webb.

Illustrations by Renée Low

The publisher wishes to thank all of the owners whose dogs are illustrated in this book, including the La Grange-Beaume family.

Greyhounds dating back to the second century AD, depicted in a well-known carving housed in the British Museum.

HISTORY OF THE

GREYHOUND

Ancient silver coins bearing the Celtic
Greyhound as ornamentation.

EARLY SIGHT HOUNDS

The Greyhound falls into the group of dogs classified as sight hounds, known also as gaze hounds, although in natural history the word "greyhound" is used to describe a whole group of similar dogs. A sight hound, of which the Greyhound is an early representative, is one that hunts its prey principally by sight. Its body is lean and powerful, with a deep chest and long limbs that provide both stamina and speed. Such hounds are adapted for finding prey in open country. Once the prey has been located, it can be overtaken by speed and endurance. Because of this special form of hunting, sight hounds historically have been found in regions where there is open countryside in North Africa, the Arabian countries, Afghanistan, Russia, Ireland and Scotland.

EARLY ANCESTORS

The Asiatic Wolf is most commonly accepted as the ancestor of the sight hounds, for no other wolves are known to have existed in areas where dogs of greyhound type originated. Large parts of the Sahara were once well watered,

Top: Celtic Greyhound, as shown on an ancient coin. Bottom: An ancient ring depicting a Celtic Greyhound killing a hare. The Celts were an ancient tribe originating in 1500 BC in Germany and spreading westward through France, Spain and Britain around 700 BC. They were conquered and absorbed by the Romans and barbarians; only Brittany and the west of the British Isles remained Celtic.

some were paid divine honors. Indeed, a war once broke out due to someone's having eaten a dog from another city. In Egypt, the dog was mourned at death, with the Egyptian people sometimes fasting and shaving their heads. A dead dog was carefully embalmed, wrapped in linen and placed in a special tomb. Mourners wailed loudly and beat themselves as an expression of grief. Conversely, Hebrews loathed the dog and were taught not to fall into the error of worshiping it as a false idol.

Greyhound from a marble relief dating from the early second century AD. Note that the dog lacks the racy build of modern Greyhounds.

supplying plentiful herds of animals and providing excellent hunting grounds for these dogs. Dogs of the chase were looked upon quite differently from others, for Mohammed permitted these. The animals captured thus were allowed to be eaten, provided that the name of Allah was uttered when the dogs were slipped to give chase.

Thanks to the ancient Egyptians' art of writing, we now have many pictures of early hounds, and even the names of many of them. Dogs were clearly venerated. Specific amounts of food had to be provided for them, and

GREEKS AND THEIR GREYHOUNDS

Sight hounds were also known to the Greeks, and many such dogs were depicted in decorative metalwork. They were also portrayed in carvings of ivory and stone, and on terracotta oil bottles, wine coolers and vases. The Greyhound was one of three large dogs used by the Greeks, the others being the Mastiff and Molossian Hound. Interestingly, Socrates speaks of snares and nets being "everywhere prohibited," from which one can deduce that

it was considered unsporting to use such hunting methods.

The Greek historian Arrian lectured on coursing and, in AD 124, gave the following description of a Greyhound bitch: "I have myself bred a hound whose eyes are the greyest of grey. A swift, hard-working, courageous, sound-footed dog, and she proves a match at any time for four hares. She is, moreover, most gentle and kindly affectioned, and never before had I a dog with such a regard for myself."

Arrian goes on to say that his

Queen Elizabeth I, hawking with Greyhounds. From Turberville's *Book of Falconrie*, 1611 edition.

foot and then the other. She also had many tones of "speech" to convey her wants. Clearly Arrian was a most considerate owner, for he also writes, "Nothing is so helpful as a soft, warm bed. It is best of all if they can sleep with a person, because it makes them more human, and because they rejoice in the company of human beings."

The *Treatise on the Greyhound*, written by Arrian, lay undiscovered in the library of the Vatican for many a long year, having been mistaken for a better known manuscript. Thankfully the treatise was eventually translated, and it was first published in English in 1831. In the treatise are many words of wisdom, among these comments about how to judge a fast, well-bred Greyhound. "First, let them stand long

bitch stayed close by his side when at home and followed him while outdoors. To remind him that she was to have her share of the food, she patted him with one

From *Icones Animalium*, 1780. The original caption reads *Canis grajus*.

Kilburgh, the son of Kilhith, as he traveled to Arthur's Court. These dogs wore broad collars, set with rubies, and they were said to have sprung about their owner like two sea-swallows.

FOREST LAWS

The Celts are clearly thought to have introduced the Greyhound to Britain from Asia, but specific dates are uncertain. Greyhounds, though, were specifically

from head to stern...let them have light and well-knit heads...Let the neck be long, rounded and supple...Broad breasts are better than narrow, and let them have shoulder blades standing apart and not fastened together...loins that are broad, strong not fleshy, but solid with sinew...flanks pliant...Rounded and fine feet are the strongest."

GREYHOUNDS IN THE BRITISH MUSEUM

One of the most famous marble sculptures, housed in the British Museum, is of two seated Grey-hounds, dating back to the second century AD. These hounds are remarkably similar to those we know today and, for those interested in the breed, a visit to the British Museum is well worthwhile.

EARLY GREYHOUNDS IN WALES

In southwestern Wales, in AD 500, two "white-breasted brindled greyhounds" ran beside Prince

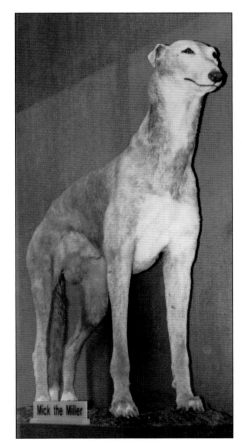

The Greyhound Mick the Miller, a racer idolized by English racegoers during his career from 1928 to 1931. He is now preserved and on display at the British Museum.

Mick the Miller

mentioned in the Forest Laws, which were made at Winchester by King Canute in 1016. A law was introduced that forbade commoners from owning Greyhounds, though freemen were allowed to keep them under certain conditions. If they lived within ten miles of the forest, the Greyhounds had to be cut at the knee so they could not hunt. Those living further away did not have to be cut, but, if they approached nearer to the forest, 12 pence was to be paid for every mile. Owners of Greyhounds found within the forest had to forfeit both the dog and ten shillings to the king.

Both the wolf and the wild boar were hunted with Greyhounds, so these dogs were both sufficiently large and powerful to cope with such prey. Before the signing of the Magna Carta (1215), there was proof that Greyhounds were held in extremely high esteem, for the destruction of such a hound was looked upon as an act "equaly criminal with the murder of a fellow man."

Greyhounds were also frequently taken in payment as money for debts owed. In 1203, a fine paid to King John consisted of 500 marks, ten horses and ten leashes of Greyhounds. Seven years later, another debt was recorded as a swift running horse and six Greyhounds.

THE BOKE OF ST. ALBANS

No book about the Greyhound would be complete without the description of the breed given in *The Boke of St. Albans*, dated 1486. This was the first sporting book ever printed in English and, although some debate surrounds the authorship, the following verse (one of several slightly different versions) is attributed to Dame Juliana Berners, believed to have been prioress of Sopewell nunnery.

A greyhound should be
    headed like a Snake,
And necked like a Drake,
Footed like a Cat,
Tailed like a Rat,
Sided like a Team,

This is the first page of *The Boke of St. Albans*, 1486.

Bestis of the chace of the swete fewte & stinkig

Ther be bestys of the chace : of the swete fewte . And tho be the Bucke . the Doo . the Beere . the Reynd the Elke . the Spytard . the Otre . and the Martron.

℃ Ther be bestis of the chace of the stynkyng fewte And thay be the Roobucke . and the Roo . the Fulmard . the Fychew . the Bauce . the Grape . the Foy . the Squyrell . the Whitrat . the Fichew . the Sot . and the Pulcatte.

℃ The namys of diuerse maner houndis

Theis be the namys of houndes . First ther is a Grehownd a Bastard . a Mengrell . a Mastyfe . a Lemor . a Spanyell . Rachys . Kenettys . Terours . Bocherls houndes . Myddyng dogges . Tryndeltayles . and Prikheryd currys . and smale ladies popis that bere a way the flees and dyuers smale fawtis .

℃ The propreteis of a goode Grehound.

A Grehounde shulde be heded like a Snake . and necked like a Drake . Foted like a Kat . Tayled like a Rat . Syded lyke a Teme . Chyned like a Beme .

℃ The first yere he most lerne to fede . The secund yere to fede hym lede . ℃ The . iij . yere he is felow lyke . The . iiij . yere ther is noon sike ℃ The . v . yere he is good Jnough The . vi . yere he shall holde the plough ℃ The vij . yere he will avayle : grete bikkys for to assayle . ℃ The . viij . yere likladill . The . ix . yere cartsadyll . ℃ And When he is com

Chined like a Bream.
The first year he must learn to
feed,
The second year to field him
lead,
The third year he is fellow-
like,
The fourth year there is none
sike,
The fifth year he is good
enough,
The sixth year he shall hold
the plough,
The seventh year he will avail
Great bitches for to assail,
The eighth year lick ladle,
The ninth year cart saddle,
And when he is comen to that
year
Have him to the tanner,
For the best hound that ever
bitch had
At nine year he is full bad.
—*Dame Juliana Berners*

COURSING AND TRACK RACING

An important reason for combining the skills of dog and man was to hunt more effectively, one assisting the other. As a result, man began to breed dogs that were constructed in such a way that they could best bring down local game, hence providing an important part of the family's diet.

The coursing breeds were developed to a large extent in the Middle East, and coursing contained a competitive element even as early as 4000 BC. This eventually led to codes of practice, something we learn of in Arrian's writings in the second century AD.

Greyhounds, like many other sight-hound breeds, have remained true to type over the

Coursing at Swaffham from *The Sporting Magazine*, 1793.

centuries. It is because of this
that many have continued to
carry out the work for which
they were originally bred and
adapted.

In Great Britain, coursing
was not conducted under established rules until the reign of
Queen Elizabeth I (1558–1603).
Responsible for drawing up the
rules, the Duke of Norfolk stipu-
lated that a hare was never to be
coursed with more than a brace

FAMOUS FANCIERS

Many famous people throughout
history have owned Greyhounds.
According to legend, Cleopatra had
coursing Greyhounds, and Greyhounds
are always depicted as the hunting
hounds of the goddess Diana. Other
prominent owners have included
Frederick the Great and Prince Albert,
of whom the lovely Greyhound Eos
was a particular favorite.

A detail from a
1436 painting by
Pisanello called
"Vision of St.
Eustace."

of Greyhounds, nor was she to be killed while "on her seat." It was also decreed that the quarry was to be given 12 score yards before the hounds were loosed so that the dogs would not leap on her as soon as she rose. Much was written about the sport in the 17th century, and Greyhounds featured prominently.

For part of her life, Queen Elizabeth I did not hunt personally, but she witnessed the coursing of deer by Greyhounds from her residence. She is recorded as having witnessed "from a turret at Cowdrey Park sixteen bucks, all having fair law, pulled down by Greyhounds upon the lawn one day after dinner." Indeed, dogs have long played a part in the history of Britain through its rulers, for London's Isle of Dogs actually derived its name from

HOUNDS AROUND THE WORLD

While the United Kingdom lays claim to the world's most famous sight hounds, namely the Greyhound, Whippet, Deerhound and Irish Wolfhound, other nations and regions have produced impressive greyhound types. Afghanistan's namesake, the Afghan Hound, Italy's Italian Greyhound and Cirneco dell'Etna, Malta's Pharaoh Hound, Spain's Ibizan Hound and Galgo Español, Iran's Saluki, Morocco's Sloughi and Zimbabwe's Rhodesian Ridgeback are counted among other recognized sighthound breeds. Further, lesser known dogs from Russia, such as the Tazy, Taigan and Chortaj, Hungary's Magyar Agar, Mali's Azawakh and Poland's Chart Polski also represent this classic greyhound type around the world.

Lord Orford's Czarina and Maria from *Rural Sports*, 1801.

being the place where Edward III (1327–1377) kept his Greyhounds and spaniels.

LORD ORFORD'S INFLUENCE ON THE BREED

During the 18th century, Lord Orford, seemingly not content with this already splendid breed, set about developing a faster Greyhound. He introduced several experimental crosses, including the Bulldog in an endeavor to increase persistence. The reason for this was that he had been impressed by the determination displayed by Bulldogs when fighting in the pit. Apart

Fullerton was sold as a puppy for a then-record sum of 850 guineas. His body now rests in Britain's Natural History Museum. The illustration is from *The Dog* by Wesley Mills, 1892.

from the Bulldog, the Deerhound, Lurcher and Italian Greyhound also were introduced into the Greyhound breed.

Initially Orford's theories were considered absurd, but soon dogs produced as a result of his breeding program were considered both the fastest and sturdiest, and hence the most efficient, running dogs. At times he was known to have kept 50 braces of Greyhounds, and it was a rule never to part with a single whelp until it had a fair and substantial trial of speed.

Upon the death of Lord Orford, the best dogs of his strain were purchased by Colonel Thornton and thus moved northward to Norfolk and Yorkshire. However, except when they were working on flat country, their

KANGAROO HOUND

Australia once boasted its own Greyhound breed known as the Kangaroo Hound, developed to hunt wallabies, dingoes and, of course, kangaroos. These dogs, heavier than a typical Greyhound, never gained the favor of the breeders and subsequently became extinct as the protection of the native Australian wildlife made the national agenda.

Greyhound with hare from the *Naturalists Library*, 1840.

success apparently fell below expectations.

With foundations laid down by Lord Orford, the first coursing club was established at Swaffham in 1776 with members confined in number to the letters of the alphabet. There was no letter "I," so membership stood at 25. Subscriptions were moderate, but there were monetary fines for non-attendance at meetings and for breaking the rules. The National Coursing Club, with its own stud book, was commenced in 1858.

The coursing Greyhound, however, is generally smaller than the Greyhound found in today's show ring, and most winners of the famous Waterloo Cup have been comparatively small. Although there used to be "park coursing," in which hares were released for the purpose, this is not now so; such release has not been permitted in England for around 100 years. In 1976, the House of Lords Select Committee found that no unnecessary suffering was caused to the hare by coursing.

Numbers of coursing Greyhounds registered far outnumber those registered with the English Kennel Club for the purposes of showing. Although from the 20th century, many consider Cornwall

The Greyhound Lauderdale from the *Illustrated Book of the Dog*, 1881.

"I AND McGRATH"

One of the most famous winners of the Greyhound world's Waterloo Cup had an audience with that great dog lover, Queen Victoria. The dog, Master McGrath, traveled to meet her by private train.

to be the original home of the show Greyhound, few were exhibited in the south of England towards the close of the 19th century. There was better participation in the classes of shows held in northern England.

Track racing developed from coursing, partly as a means of controlling the crowds of onlookers at coursing meetings. An artificial lure was developed and first used in England in 1876. This was a stuffed rabbit that ran on a long rail, but it did not prove popular. Enclosed coursing in parks was much more in favor. Not until the early 20th century did track racing became popular, following the development of a lure that could be run around a track. The first racing stadium was created in Manchester in 1926.

Many well-known racing Greyhounds will go down in the annals of history, among them Fullerton, who was sold to his

owner Colonel North for a record price of 850 guineas. Fullerton won 31 of his 33 races, including the Waterloo Cup in 1889, 1890 and 1891, and sharing the honors in 1892.

Mick the Miller was another Greyhound idolized by millions of racegoers in Britain in the 1920s and '30s. The bodies of both of these great hounds are preserved in the British Museum.

Greyhound named Age of Gold, bred and owned by F. Alexander, Esq. From the painting by Lilian Cheviot in the *New Book of the Dog* by Robert Leigh, 1907.

AN ALLURING NOTION

In Australia, mechanical lure racing was pioneered by Frederick Swindell, an American who had moved to the country in 1927. As a result, the Greyhound Coursing Association was established that same year. A mechanical lure circuit was permitted on the site now known as Harold Park.

THE NAME "GREYHOUND"

There is much conjecture about the origin of the name "Greyhound." It has been spelled variously as "grehounde," "griehounde," "grayhounde," "graihound," "grewhound" and "grewnd." One early authority considered that it was drawn from the ancient English word *grech* or *greg*, meaning "dog."

This may be so, but others believe that it relates to the color of the breed in its early days. However, there is no evidence to suggest that grey (spelled also as "gray," "grai" and "grei") was the prevailing color, the breed also being found in sandy red, brindle, pale yellow and white.

Another theory is that the name implies "Gallic hound," giving rise to the conjecture that it actually originated in Gaul. Followers of this theory consider that the word can be translated as *gradus* in Latin, meaning "degree," because it exceeded the speed of other dogs. "Gree" was certainly used to represent the word "degree." A further theory worthy of consideration is that the word *grew* was often used for "Greek," thus indicating a connection with Greece.

GREYHOUNDS IN THE AMERICAS

The Greyhound arrived in the Americas with the Spanish in the 16th century, as well as with early British colonists. These dogs were used on America's Great Plains, useful for protecting crops from devastation by rabbits, and live-stock from danger from coyotes. Although they hunted a variety of game, they were most highly renowned for their excellence in chasing hare and rabbit.

In 1885, the Greyhound was one of the first six hound breeds

THE FIRST CRUFTS BEST

The year 1928 was the first year in which Crufts made an official Best in Show award open to any entrant. Hitherto there had been a prize for Best Champion, but not Best in Show. The first winner of this important award was a Greyhound, Primely Sceptre, and this title was won again by Greyhounds in 1934 and 1956.

to be registered with the American Kennel Club (AKC), but this was the only breed to represent the sight hounds.

Formed in 1907, the Greyhound Club of America (GCA) became the breed's national parent club, being recognized by the AKC two years later. The breed had been exhibited for over 25 years by this point, including an entry of 16 dogs in the 1880 Westminster Kennel Club show in New York City. The GCA's first national specialty took place in October of 1923 on grounds owned by fancier J. S. Shipps of Long Island. Both conformation and coursing were included in this first event. With the exception of a few years, the specialty on the East Coast has occurred annually and attracted fair numbers of American fanciers. A West Coast specialty began in 1968, set into motion by the breed's growing

popularity on that shore.

Since the 1920s, the Greyhound in America has been involved with track racing, but the breed still also is kept both as a sporting hound and as a companion. Clearly the Greyhound is synonymous with speed, and even the famous Greyhound

The popular actress Annette Crosbie (left) befriends a Greyhound rescue dog at Britain's Crufts Dog Show.

A racing Greyhound in action. The dog's front legs are taped for support.

buses carry the breed's name, presumably to convey the efficiency, speed and endurance of their renowned service.

SHOW GREYHOUNDS IN EUROPE

With the Greyhound's being such an endearing and well-mannered breed, it is perhaps surprising that they are not represented in stronger numbers on the show bench. At a recent International Championship Show in Holland, there were only 15 Greyhounds entered, compared to 48 Whippets and 46 Afghan Hounds.

In Britain, at a recent Crufts show, there were 73 Greyhounds entered, a significantly higher number than at most shows on the Continent. However, this is still far fewer than the other well-known sight hound breeds, with Whippets topping 300 for the sake of comparison.

You have to be fairly tall to have your Greyhound stretch for a treat.

Few Greyhounds are shown at major dog shows. They are, however, becoming more and more common as pets, as an increasing number of people opt to make retired racers part of their lives.

CHARACTERISTICS OF THE

GREYHOUND

A well-constructed Greyhound is a truly beautiful animal. The breed's graceful lines, clearly seen thanks to the smooth coat, are visible for all to see—it's a veritable feast for the eyes of any true lover of sight hounds.

The Greyhound is a classic sight hound. Its grace, symmetry and tremendous speed have undoubtedly helped in endearing many to the breed through countless centuries. This splendid breed has won royal favor and has been a symbol of aristocracy, and, in today's changing world, the Greyhound has become well-known and loved by all.

Although a thing of great beauty and undeniable quality within the canine race, the Greyhound is not a status symbol. Dagmar Kenis-Pordham, a Greyhound breeder held in high regard throughout the world, described the breed as being "as dignified and graceful as its heritage." I cannot better that description. Mrs. Kenis-Pordham also recommends that people think of the Greyhound as "a piece of history, a very alive antique." Surely, that says it all.

PERSONALITY
The Greyhound makes a great companion dog, for this is an affectionate, gentle and faithful breed with an even temper and quiet disposition. The breed is

Some great racers look like flying machines! Although an instant association is usually made between Greyhounds and racing, racing is only a small part of what this wonderful breed is all about.

dog, which makes him a quick learner. He is also a pack dog. This means that a Greyhound is quite prepared to accept a human into his pack and, if sensibly managed, to treat that human as the pack leader.

A thoroughly expressive dog in his character, the Greyhound has a delightfully relaxed demeanor. However, Greyhounds, especially those that have been retired from track racing, have both the instinct and ability to chase anything that moves. It is therefore essential that cats and other small animals that could provide easy targets be kept well out of harm's way.

GREYHOUNDS AND OTHER PETS
Many Greyhounds, if socialized carefully with other family pets from an early age, are able to live alongside them in perfect harmony. However, even though

also said to have quite a sense of humor! However, owners of Greyhounds must recognize that this is a dog with remarkable stamina, speed and endurance. Fastest members of the breed are capable of running at over 45 miles per hour—only the cheetah can top the Greyhound for speed. This said, the only households that should really take on a Greyhound are those in which the family has the time, energy and space to allow this breed the exercise it requires to live a happy, fulfilled life.

The Greyhound is a sensitive and intelligent

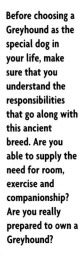

Before choosing a Greyhound as the special dog in your life, make sure that you understand the responsibilities that go along with this ancient breed. Are you able to supply the need for room, exercise and companionship? Are you really prepared to own a Greyhound?

your Greyhound may have accepted the family's cat, the same sentiment is unlikely to apply when a neighbor's cat has the audacity to venture into your Greyhound's yard!

GREYHOUNDS AND CHILDREN

Any owner who has dogs and children must teach the latter to respect their canine friends and to treat them gently. Greyhounds are tolerant dogs and most get along well with children, especially if they have been sensibly introduced while the dog is still young. Nonetheless, you should always keep in mind that a Greyhound is a big dog, and the limits of his tolerance should never be put to the test. Careful supervision is the key to building a successful relationship between child and dog.

Despite their large size, some Greyhounds refuse to believe that they're not lap dogs!

PHYSICAL CHARACTERISTICS

SIZE

The Greyhound is undoubtedly a large dog, show dogs standing between 28 to 30 inches, with bitches 27 to 28 inches. Racing Greyhounds tend to be significantly smaller.

The Greyhound's size, coupled with his construction, makes for a dog with both form and function. The breed is the fastest and one of the most elegant in all of dogdom.

This breed carries very little body fat, and weight generally ranges somewhere between 60 and 70 lb, although the weight of a track Greyhound usually averages rather less than a show dog.

The breed's very size, coupled with its construction, makes Greyhounds able to move swiftly around the home. They are quite capable of reaching virtually anything to which they take a fancy, so sensible management and control are important. Although many Greyhounds spend a lot of time outdoors, properly trained Greyhounds make wonderful companions to join in family life around the home. A Greyhound can, and does, lie outstretched and take up a vast amount of room on your living room floor, but he can just as easily tuck himself up comfortably in a corner or on an armchair. However the dog chooses to relax, you can be assured that the very sight of a Greyhound enjoying quiet time in the comfort of your home is quite lovely.

COAT AND COLOR

A Greyhound's coat is short and smooth, with fine strands of hair close together, and should not be sparse. Although a Greyhound sheds, this can be kept easily under control with simple grooming and general care.

The colors of this breed are many and varied, and dog-show judges hold no preference for any color; in fact, the AKC's breed standard states that color is

---

WEIGH HOUND

Provided you are strong enough, perhaps the easiest method of weighing your Greyhound puppy is on the bathroom scales. First weigh yourself alone, then a second time while holding the pup in your arms. Deduct one from the other to obtain the accurate weight of your puppy.

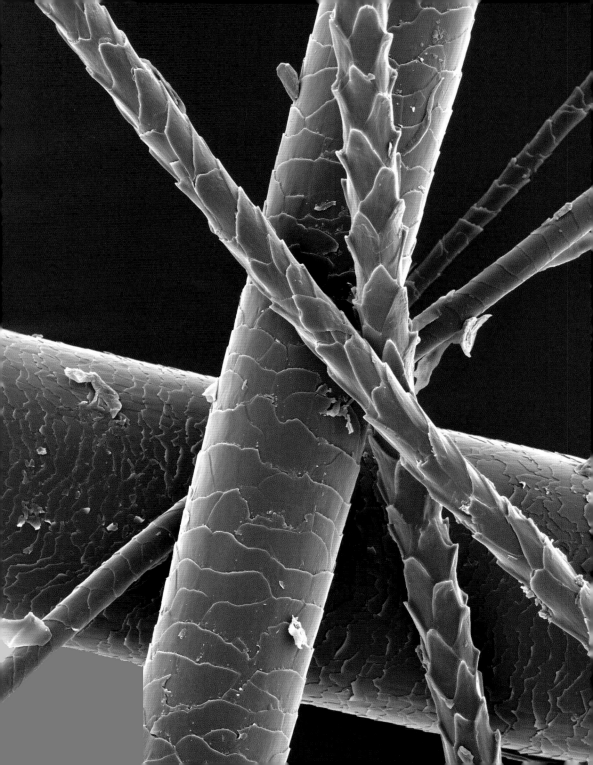

"immaterial." Thus it is that Greyhounds are found in a wide variety, ranging from white through black, in solid colors and patterns of color broken with white. This variety of colors is just another interesting aspect of this splendid breed.

LIFESPAN
Clearly, when taking a Greyhound into your home, the principal aim will be that the dog remains with you for his entire life. Although a tall breed, the Greyhound is not as heavily built as the giant breeds, which tend to live relatively short lives. Hence, a healthy Greyhound can be expected to live on average for about 12 years, sometimes longer.

TAKING ON A RETIRED RACING GREYHOUND
Show Greyhounds are still few and far between, with about 200 new puppies registered with the American Kennel Club each year. On the other hand, racing Greyhounds are plentiful and, once their useful lives on the track are over, many an ex-racer seeks a new, long-term, loving home.

Like their show relations, racing Greyhounds are quiet yet mentally very alert. Numerous

Facing page: Greyhound hairs, which appear healthy. The cuticle (outer covering of the hair) is uniform with just a little dandruff. Enlargement is 250 times actual size.

Greyhounds appear in many interesting colors and color combinations other than gray.

owners say how wonderful they are to keep as pets around the home. Sadly, many such dogs reach an all-too-early death if not re-homed, as they find themselves put to sleep well before their time is due. Others, though, live well into old age and adapt to their new homes admirably, perhaps all the more grateful for the love and much-needed attention they receive in their advancing years.

Clearly not all homes are suitable for retired racing Greyhounds. Their owners should enjoy taking their dogs on long walks, to which they are understandably accustomed, and careful consideration must be given to other family pets, especially cats!

HEALTH CONSIDERATIONS

Because so few show Greyhounds are bred, the available gene pool is undeniably small.

TO THE RESCUE

Unfortunately, many racing Greyhounds are not given the opportunity to live out their full lives after their careers on the racing track are over. Greyhound rescue does great work in many countries, and many lovely dogs are re-homed through the dedicated efforts of adoption organizations.

Thus, it is fortunate that the foundation stock was originally sound, making this a breed free from known hereditary problems. The Greyhound is indeed one of the healthiest of all breeds.

Nonetheless, like all dogs, some Greyhounds do suffer from illnesses and it is only fair to owners and to the dogs in question that attention is brought to these. Awareness of any problems that may possibly arise can only help owners to know when it is necessary to seek veterinary advice.

CANCER

Since the 1990s, the occurrence of cancer in Greyhounds (primarily ex-racers) has been unusually high. Osteosarcoma, affecting the bones of large-breed dogs, is the most aggressive cancer occurring at a frequent rate. Signs are swelling and limping, requiring immediate veterinary attention. Other cancers cited in Greyhounds include fibrosarcoma, hemangiosarcoma, mast cell tumors, breast cancer, liver cancer and colon cancer. Concerned breeders have been making great strides in preventing the spread of cancer in the breed, though much more effort is still warranted.

Although it is not proven that Greyhounds are any more susceptible to bone cancer than

other breeds, there have been many such cases reported, especially in former racers. Owners should therefore always be on the lookout for any early signs of bone cancer, one of which may be lameness in a leg.

Sensitivities of the Breed

Greyhounds, like other sight hounds, have a very low proportion of body fat in relation to their size. In fact, the average fat content on a Grey-hound's body is only about 16%, whereas this is nearer to 35% in many similar-sized dogs of other breeds. Added to this, the Grey-hound's liver metabolizes toxins out of the bloodstream at a rather slow rate

compared with other dogs of similar size.

As a result, anesthesia is one of various medications to which Greyhounds are sensitive, so it is important to discuss this with your vet prior to surgery. Special anesthetics can be used that are more suitable for the Greyhound and other similar breeds, and it is recommended that barbiturates be avoided.

Dealing with Fleas

It may come as some surprise that flea collars that contain long-lasting pesticides can be harmful to Greyhounds. Organophosphates, which are harmful to many dogs,

Many owners of retired racers will attest to the fact that their dogs "made themselves at home" with no problems!

This is what a champion show Greyhound looks like. This is Hound Group Winner Eng. Ch. Ballalyn's Foggy at Mist-weave, owned by Savage & Savage-Hargreaves.

are particularly deleterious to the Greyhound. Certainly any flea control that involves releasing chemicals into the bloodstream should be avoided. Of course, it is important that your dog should be entirely free from fleas, so stringency is important. There are safe products on the market, so owners should discuss with their vets what is on offer before selecting what they consider is the safest flea control available.

EXCESS WEIGHT

Greyhounds that were once in racing condition but have been subsequently retired may well put on excess fat when muscle tone has been lost. All Grey-

The Greyhound is one of the healthiest breeds around and is nearly free from hereditary diseases.

hounds, especially older ones, should always be kept trim. There are really no adequate excuses for not noticing that your Greyhound is putting on too much weight!

BLOAT

Bloat, also known as gastric torsion, is a life-threatening disease that affects many deep-chested breeds. Effectively the stomach actually flips over, requiring immediate veterinary attention to avoid fatal consequences, which occur quickly.

As a measure of protection against bloat, a Greyhound should not be fed immediately after exercise, nor should he be exercised for at least an hour before or following a meal. A Greyhound should also have his food and water bowls placed higher than ground level so that he does not have to stoop to reach them.

A symptom of bloat is a distended abdomen, together with restlessness and unproductive efforts to vomit. A Greyhound suffering from bloat must be brought to a vet immediately; death will result quickly if no corrective action is taken.

HYGROMA

When large dogs like Greyhounds lie regularly on hard flooring, fluid-filled lumps can appear on bony prominences. This is actually Nature's way of protecting

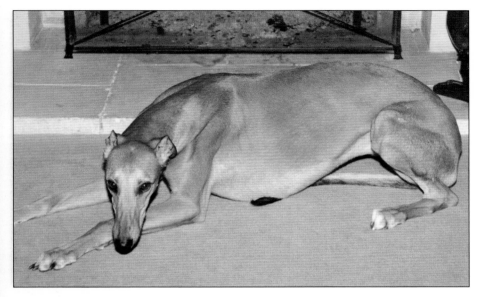

When Greyhounds lie on hard surfaces, they might develop fluid-filled sites on the bony prominences. Bring these to the attention of your vet, who might suggest a soft pillow upon which your pet can rest.

the fine skin from the bone beneath, but sometimes these hygromas can become inflamed or ulcerated. Although they look unsightly, veterinary attention coupled with a change to softer bedding usually can rectify the problem.

HYPOTHYROIDISM

Some Greyhounds do seem to suffer from hypothyroidism. An early symptom is bilateral hair loss, usually on the back or neck. When coat has been lost, the skin becomes noticeably thicker and darker. Hypothyroidism can have long-term effects and is sometimes connected with diabetes. Urgent veterinary advice and relevant blood testing is the best course of action to help such a

dog lead as long and comfortable a life as possible.

TEETH

Although Greyhounds usually have strong teeth, it is always important to pay close attention to the care of teeth and gums. This way, your Greyhound will remain as healthy as possible with consequent prevention of decay, infection and resultant loss of teeth.

Infection in the gums may not just stop there. The bacteria from such an infection is carried through the bloodstream, the result of which can be diseases of the liver, kidney, heart and joints. This is all the more reason to realize that efficient dental care is of utmost importance throughout any dog's life.

GREYHOUND

The breed standard for the Greyhound is effectively a "blueprint" for the breed. It sets down the various points of the dog in words, enabling a visual picture to be conjured up in the mind of the reader. However, this is more easily said than done. Not only do standards vary from country to country but people's interpretations of breed standards vary also. It is this difference of interpretation that makes judges select different dogs for top honors, for their opinions differ as to which dog most closely fits the breed standard. That is neither to say that a good dog does not win regularly under different judges, nor that an inferior dog may rarely even be placed at a show, at least not among quality competition.

The breed standard given here is that authorized by the American Kennel Club (AKC). It is followed by the author's commentary on the standard.

THE AMERICAN KENNEL CLUB STANDARD FOR THE GREYHOUND

Head: Long and narrow, fairly wide between the ears, scarcely perceptible stop, little or no development of nasal sinuses, good length of muzzle, which should be powerful without coarseness. Teeth very strong and even in front.

Ears: Small and fine in texture, thrown back and folded, except when excited, when they are semi-pricked.

Eyes: Dark, bright, intelligent, indicating spirit.

Neck: Long, muscular, without throatiness, slightly arched, and widening gradually into the shoulder.

COLORS OF THE HOUND

While the AKC standard simply states that the Greyhound's color is immaterial, the English standard provides us with a list of possible colors in the breed. These include "black, white, red, blue, fawn, fallow, brindle or any of these colors broken with white."

THE GREAT FOOT DEBATE

The subject of feet in the breed has always been a subject for debate. The English standard is fairly explicit and the cat-like foot as described by Dame Juliana Berners is not mentioned. However, in the American standard one finds the clarification that the Greyhound's feet should be "Hard and close, rather more hare than catfeet." Both standards say that the toes should be well arched.

Shoulders: Placed as obliquely as possible, muscular without being loaded.

Forelegs: Perfectly straight, set well into the shoulders, neither turned in nor out, pasterns strong.

Chest: Deep, and as wide as consistent with speed, fairly well-sprung ribs.

Back: Muscular and broad.

The standard by which Greyhounds are judged does not take into account racing ability. A champion racing dog might not be eligible for a championship in the show ring. Pictured here is a champion show dog.

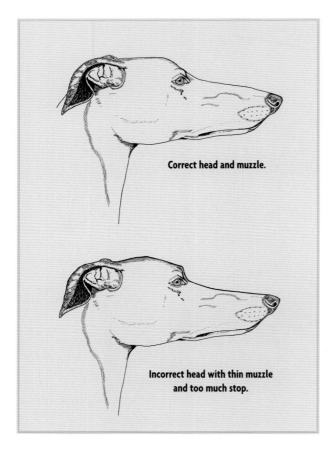

Correct head and muzzle.

Incorrect head with thin muzzle
and too much stop.

Tail: Long, fine and tapering with a slight upward curve.

Coat: Short, smooth and firm in texture.

Color: Immaterial.

Weight: Dogs, 65 to 70 pounds; bitches 60 to 65 pounds.

SIZE AND GAIT

Since the AKC standard does not give the reader any indication of the height or gait (movement) of the breed, it is helpful to look at the English standard for this information. The Kennel Club standard states: "Size: Ideal height: dogs: 71–76 cm (28–30 in); bitches: 68–71 cm (27–28 in)." The AKC standard provides information only on the weight of the Greyhound, ranging from 60 to 70 lb. The English standard tells us that the Greyhound's gait should be a "Straight, low reaching, free stride enabling the ground to be covered at great speed (with the) hindlegs coming well under body giving great propulsion." For a breed that is world-famous for its swift movement, it seems a rather strange omission on the part of the breed club and AKC to omit this description.

Loins: Good depth of muscle, well arched, well cut up in the flanks.

Hindquarters: Long, very muscular and powerful, wide and well let down, well-bent stifles. Hocks well bent and rather close to ground, wide but straight fore and aft.

Feet: Hard and close, rather more hare than catfeet, well knuckled up with good strong claws.

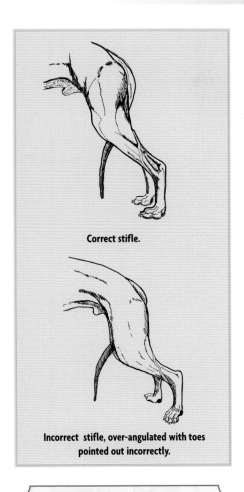

Correct stifle.

Incorrect stifle, over-angulated with toes pointed out incorrectly.

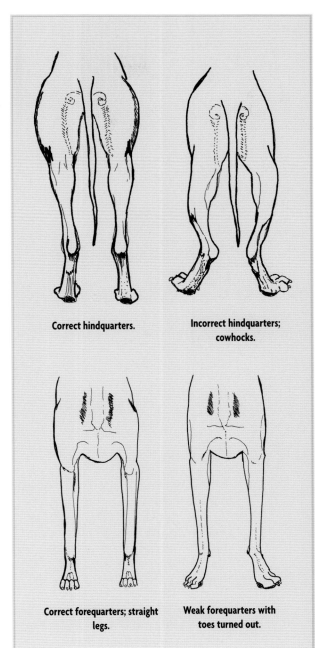

Correct hindquarters.

Incorrect hindquarters; cowhocks.

Correct forequarters; straight legs.

Weak forequarters with toes turned out.

SCALE OF POINTS

General symmetry and quality	10
Head and neck	20
Chest and shoulders	20
Back	10
Quarters	20
Legs and feet	20
TOTAL	**100**

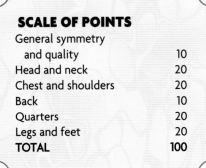

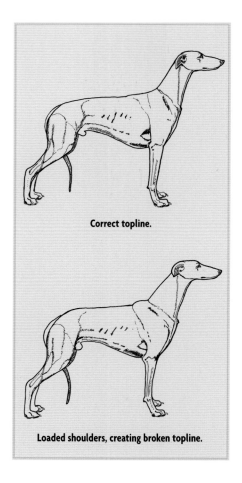

Correct topline.

Loaded shoulders, creating broken topline.

COMMENTARY ON THE BREED STANDARD

Although a great deal can be learned from the breed standard, only by seeing good-quality, typical specimens can one really learn to appreciate the breed's merits. Therefore, readers interested in showing their Greyhounds should watch other dogs being exhibited and learn as much as possible from established breeders and exhibitors.

It is helpful to attend judges' seminars when available. Here the finer points of the breed can be explained fully and discussed. There is usually a dog, or perhaps a handful, available for demonstration purposes, and there may be an opportunity for participants to gain hands-on experience, giving a valuable insight into the structure of the animal.

A few elaborations on the description of the breed are worthy of comment here. First, the Greyhound is not a finely built dog, although it is understandable that bitches should be more feminine in appearance than their male counterparts. The breed should have generous proportions, referring to body and shape, for this is a breed constructed on long lines, one in which there is a continuous, smoothly curving line from the head to the very tip of the tail. The Greyhound's brisket is deep, and there is good tuck-up flowing into hindquarters with well-bent stifles, so the underline, too, is one of graceful curves.

Muscular power is important in the Greyhound. This muscle should be elastic and supple, but a dog such as this should not be overly muscled. Indeed, the breed standard says that the shoulders should be "muscular without being loaded." On the other hand, because the Greyhound should have both stamina and endurance, the dog must not carry too much weight; rather, he should be in lean, muscular condition.

Considered a mark of quality, the fine coat is considered to be one of the points that sets the show Greyhound apart from the racer. Another important word that repeats itself in the breed standard is "long." Indeed the Greyhound has sometimes been called the "long dog." The word "long" describes many parts of this splendid hound: the head, neck, back, legs and tail. And, although couched in different terms, the Greyhound's stride is also long.

For the work he has been expected to do over generations, it is imperative that the Greyhound is a balanced dog. Every part of the body should be in proportion to the rest and should fit gracefully together. To move well, both the front and hindquarters must be equally matched in angulation, and the chest and rib cage deep and capacious enough to adequately house the heart and lungs. The loins need to be powerful and arched.

Lastly we come to color, which, it has to be said, can all too easily deceive the eye. Darker colored dogs can give the

The speed and grace of Greyhounds have been compared with those of a gazelle.

optical illusion that they are rather finer in bone than the white or light-colored dogs, but feeling the bone and skeletal structure will give a truer impression. Because many Greyhounds are parti-colored, meaning white with another color, the actual markings can also serve to make a dog look shorter than he is. A heavy dark marking set on the side of a dog amid a white background can serve to give a slightly shorter bodily appearance than is really the case. So we know that, although so much of a Greyhound can be seen from the ringside, judges should also allow their hands to feel the construction of the dog in order to truly appreciate the merits of this wonderful breed.

GREYHOUND

While there are thousands of Greyhound owners in the United States, most of them never met their beloved dogs as puppies. The majority of breeders in the US breed for racing-dog kennels and not for show and pet homes. Potential owners should contact the American Kennel Club for a representative of the Greyhound Club of America (GCA). The GCA also is online at www.grey-houndclubofamerica.org. The GCA is able to recommend breeders of pet and show puppies. These professional breeders are a dedicated and knowledgeable band of Grey-hound lovers who are willing to help newcomers to the breed and to recommend litters. Since there are so few breeders in the country, most breeders know one another and are willing to work together to fill the demand for puppies, which is actually pretty limited.

If you are interested in a puppy Greyhound, as opposed to a rescue retiree, you should attend a dog show in your area. It's easy to find a dog show by looking in the newspapers or one of the dog periodicals, or by

ARE YOU PREPARED?
Unfortunately, when a puppy is bought by someone who does not take into consideration the time and attention that dog ownership requires, it is the puppy who suffers when he is either abandoned or placed in a shelter by a frustrated owner. So all of the "home-work" you do in preparation for your pup's arrival will benefit you both. The more informed you are, the more you will know what to expect and the better equipped you will be to handle the ups and downs of raising a puppy. Hopefully, everyone in the household is willing to do his part in raising and caring for the pup. The anticipation of owning a dog often brings a lot of promises from excited family members: "I will walk him every day," "I will feed him," "I will house-train him," etc., but these things take time and effort, and promises can easily be forgotten once the novelty of the new pet has worn off.

Once you've decided to own a puppy and done all of your "home-work," you're ready for the exciting part...choosing your pup!

visiting the AKC online (www.akc.org). At a dog show, you can meet exhibitors and breeders who are serious about producing top-quality puppies for the purpose of showing. Of course, most litters contain 20% show-worthy pups, and 80% pet-quality pups. A Greyhound litter of ten puppies, therefore, may produce two (three, if you're lucky or really good) show-qual-ity pups. The other seven or eight puppies will need good pet homes. Approach the handler whose dog you like the best and find out as much as can about the breeder and the line. The show catalog is a valuable tool to find out about the breeders, the differ-ent lines of Greyhounds, the names of the kennels or prefixes and popular sires and dams.

Since Greyhounds are not a popular breed at dog shows, there is the chance that you will get to the show and find no Greyhounds at all. In this case, you should talk to the breeders of the other sight hounds (like Whippets, Scottish Deerhounds, Borzoi) to see if any of those handlers know folk in Grey-hounds. Another option is to visit a lure-coursing event where all the whole sight-hound frater-nity shows up to compete with their dogs or even just to observe the breathtaking sight of these dogs in full flight. These events are more exciting than dog shows and can lead you to some real diehard sight-hound fanciers.

Meeting the dam and litter is an important part of the decision process! Make sure that the kennel is clean and that all dogs and pups are healthy. You'll also have a wonderful opportunity to observe the pups' personalities.

TEMPERAMENT COUNTS

Your selection of a good puppy can be determined by your needs. A show potential or a good pet? It is your choice. Every puppy, however, should be of good temperament. Although show-quality puppies are bred and raised with emphasis on physical conformation, responsible breeders strive for equally good temperament. Do not buy from a breeder who concentrates solely on physical beauty at the expense of personality.

Once you have contacted and met a breeder or two and made your choice about which breeder is best suited to your needs, it's time to visit the litter. Keep in mind that many top breeders have waiting lists. Sometimes new owners have to wait a year or more for a puppy. If you are really committed to the breeder whom you've selected, then you will wait (and hope for an early arrival!). If not, you may have to go with to another breeder.

Breeders commonly allow visitors to see the litter by

around the fifth or sixth week, and puppies leave for their new homes between the eighth and tenth week. Breeders who permit their puppies to leave early are more interested in your money than in their puppies' well-being. Puppies need to learn the rules of the trade from their dams, and most dams continue teaching the pups manners and dos and don'ts until around the eighth week. Breeders spend significant amounts of time with the Greyhound toddlers so that they are able to interact with the "other species," i.e., humans. Given the long history that dogs and humans have, bonding between the two species is natural but must be nurtured. A well-bred, well-socialized Greyhound pup wants nothing more than to be near you and to please you.

ADOPTING AN EX-RACER

Given the thousands of Greyhounds retired each year, many

> ### PUPPY APPEARANCE
>
> Your puppy should have a well-fed appearance but not a distended abdomen, which may indicate worms or incorrect feeding, or both. The body should be firm, with a solid feel. The skin of the abdomen should be pale pink and clean, without signs of scratching or rash. Check the hind legs to see if the dewclaws have been removed, if any were present at birth.
>
> Also check the bite of your selected puppy to be sure that it is neither overshot or undershot. This may not be too noticeable on a young puppy, but the breeder can help you predict how the jaws will develop.

owners opt to adopt adult ex-racers instead of purchasing puppies. There are over 50 race-tracks in the US, and each of these businesses "retire" or eutha-nize older dogs that can't keep up with the young "stallions." There are many Greyhound rescue

The care and feeding of racing dogs is a science in itself. Most racers are super-vised by veteri-narians who specialize in racing dogs.

groups in the country that are dedicated to placing these worthy athletes in caring homes. As many as 150 rescue centers exist, from large facilities like Greyhound Friends, The Greyhound Project and Greyhound Rescue Inc., to small home-run adoption kennels. There are also regional centers that concentrate on a two- or three-state area.

If you are interested in adopting an ex-racer, you should contact one of these organizations for information. Be prepared to fill out an application that asks you many pertinent questions to help the agency decide whether or not you are a suitable candidate. If you are fortunate enough to be approved, you will find that your new adopted "child" is a sweet and gentle creature who is fairly adaptable to home life. Keep in mind that racing Greyhounds have limited interaction with people and are not familiar ordinary household things (like steps, glass doors, TVs, cats and so on). Temperament and behavior varies considerably from dog to dog. Some ex-racers are more demonstrative than others, some like children and accept other pets and some adjust miraculously to "all the comforts of home." They will require close supervision at first, will need basic training and will need to be instructed on the house rules. With patience and common sense, an ex-racer can soon become a valued member of your family, a rewarding pet whose life you will literally have saved.

PICKING A PUPPY

So, you have decided upon the purchase of a puppy. You've decided which characteristics

PEDIGREE VS. REGISTRATION CERTIFICATE

Too often new owners are confused between these two important documents. Your puppy's pedigree, essentially a family tree, is a written record of a dog's genealogy of three generations or more. The pedigree will show you the names as well as performance titles of all dogs in your pup's background. Your breeder must provide you with a registration application, with his part properly filled out. You must complete the application and send it to the AKC with the proper fee. Every puppy must come from a litter that has been AKC-registered by the breeder, born in the USA and from a sire and dam that are also registered with the AKC.

The seller must provide you with complete records to identify the puppy. The AKC requires that the seller provide the buyer with the following: breed; sex, color and markings; date of birth; litter number (when available); names and registration numbers of the parents; breeder's name; and date sold or delivered.

you want in a family or show dog and what type of dog will best fit into your life, and you've chosen to raise a Greyhound youngster. If you have selected a breeder, you have gone a step further—you have done your research and found a responsible, conscientious person who breeds quality Greyhounds and who should be a reliable source of help as you and your puppy adjust to life together. If you have observed a litter in action, you have obtained a firsthand look at the dynamics of a puppy "pack" and, thus, you should have learned about each pup's

PET INSURANCE

Just like you can insure your car, your house and your own health, you likewise can insure your dog's health. Investigate a pet insurance policy by talking to your vet. Depending on the age of your dog, the breed and the kind of coverage you desire, your policy can be very affordable. Most policies cover accidental injuries, poisoning and thousands of medical problems and illnesses, including cancers. Some carriers also offer routine care and immunization coverage.

Puppies are naturally curious and should eagerly approach visitors. Be wary of the overly cautious pup who seems to be nervous or afraid.

individual personality—perhaps you have even found one that particularly appeals to you.

However, even if you have not yet found the puppy of your dreams, observing pups will help you learn to recognize certain behavior and to determine what a pup's behavior indicates about his temperament. You will be able to pick out which pups are the leaders, which ones are less outgoing, which ones are confident, which ones are shy, playful, friendly, aggressive, etc. Equally as important, you will learn to recognize what a healthy pup should look and act like. All of these things will help you in your search, and when you find the Greyhound that was meant for you, you will know it!

Researching your breed, selecting a responsible breeder and observing as many pups as possible are all important steps on the way to dog ownership. It may seem like a lot of effort…and you have not even taken the pup home yet! Remember, though, you cannot be too careful when it comes to deciding on the type of dog you want and finding out about your prospective pup's background. Buying a puppy is not—or *should* not be—just another whimsical purchase. This is one instance in which you actually do get to choose your own

ARE YOU A FIT OWNER?
If the breeder from whom you are buying a puppy asks you a lot of personal questions, do not be insulted. Such a breeder wants to be sure that you will be a fit provider for his puppy.

family! You may be thinking that buying a puppy should be fun—it should not be so serious and so much work. Keep in mind that your puppy is not a cuddly stuffed toy or decorative lawn ornament, but a creature that will become a real member of your family. You will come to realize that, while buying a puppy is a pleasurable and exciting endeavor, it is not something to be taken lightly. Relax...the fun will start when the pup comes home!

Always keep in mind that a puppy is nothing more than a baby in a furry disguise...a baby who is virtually helpless in a human world and who trusts his owner for fulfillment of his basic needs for survival. In addition to food, water and shelter, your pup needs care, protection, guidance and love. If you are not prepared to commit to this, then you are not ready to own any dog.

"Wait a minute," you say. "How hard could this be? All of my neighbors own dogs and they seem to be doing just fine. Why should I have to worry about all of this?" Well, you should not worry about it; in fact, you will probably find that once your Greyhound pup gets used to his new home, he will fall into his place in the family quite naturally. But it never hurts to emphasize the commitment of

dog ownership. With some time and patience, it is really not too difficult to raise a curious and exuberant Greyhound pup to be a well-adjusted and well-mannered adult dog—a dog that could be your most loyal friend.

PREPARING PUPPY'S PLACE IN YOUR HOME

Researching your breed and finding a breeder are only two aspects of the "homework" you will have to do before taking your Greyhound puppy home. You will also have to prepare your home and family for the new addition. Much as you would prepare a nursery for a newborn baby, you will need to designate a place in your home that will be the puppy's own. How you prepare your home will depend on how much freedom the dog will be allowed.

YOUR SCHEDULE . . .
If you lead an erratic, unpredictable life, with daily or weekly changes in your work requirements, consider the problems of owning a puppy. The new puppy has to be fed regularly, socialized (loved, petted, handled, introduced to other people) and, most importantly, allowed to go outdoors for house-training. As the dog gets older, he can be more tolerant of deviations in his feeding and relief schedule.

Whatever you decide, you must ensure that he has a place that he can "call his own."

When you bring your new puppy into your home, you are bringing him into what will become his home as well. Obviously, you did not buy a puppy so that he could take control of your home, but in order for a puppy to grow into a stable, well-adjusted dog, he has to feel comfortable in his surroundings. Remember, he is leaving the warmth and security of his mother and littermates, as well as the familiarity of the only place he has ever known, so it is important to make his transition as easy as possible. By preparing a place in your home for the puppy, you are making him feel as welcome as possible in a strange new place. It should not take him long to get used to it, but the sudden shock of being transplanted is somewhat traumatic for a young pup. Imagine how a small child would feel in the same situation—that is how your puppy must be feeling. It is up to you to reassure him and to let him know, "Little fellow, you are going to like it here!"

WHAT YOU SHOULD BUY

CRATE

To someone unfamiliar with the use of crates in dog training, it may seem like punishment to shut a dog in a crate, but this is not the case at all. Most breeders advocate crate training and recommend crates as preferred tools for puppies and ex-racers alike. Many racing Greyhounds will be used to crates from their track days. Crates are not cruel—crates have many humane and highly effective uses in dog care and training. For example, crate training is a very popular and very successful housebreaking method, a crate can keep your dog safe during travel and, perhaps most importantly, a crate provides your dog with a place of his own in your home. It serves as a "doggie bedroom" of sorts—your Greyhound can curl up in his crate when he wants to sleep or when he just needs a break. Many dogs sleep in their crates overnight. When lined with soft bedding and with a favorite chew toy inside, a crate becomes a cozy pseudo-den for your dog. Like his ancestors, he too will seek out the

QUALITY FOOD
The cost of food must be mentioned. All dogs need a good-quality food with an adequate supply of protein to develop their bones and muscles properly. Most dogs are not picky eaters but, unless fed properly, can quickly succumb to skin problems.

comfort and retreat of a den—you just happen to be providing him with something a little more luxurious than his early ancestors enjoyed.

As far as purchasing a crate, the type that you buy is up to you. It will most likely be one of the two most popular types: wire or fiberglass. There are advantages and disadvantages to each type. For example, a wire crate is more open, allowing the air to flow through and affording the dog a view of what is going on around him, while a fiberglass

PHOTO COURTESY OF DOSKOCIL

You should be able to find a large variety of crates at your local pet shop. You will require the largest size crate available because it must house your Greyhound when he is fully grown.

CRATE-TRAINING TIPS

During crate training, you should partition off the section of the crate in which the pup stays. If he is given too big an area, this will hinder your training efforts. Crate training is based on the fact that a dog does not like to soil his sleeping quarters, so it is ineffective to keep a pup in an area that is so big that he can eliminate in one end and get far enough away from it to sleep. Also, you want to make the crate den-like for the pup. Blankets and a favorite toy will make the crate cozy for the small pup; as he grows, you may want to evict some of his "roommates" to make more room. It will take some coaxing at first, but be patient. Given some time to get used to it, your pup will adapt to his new home-within-a-home quite nicely.

crate is sturdier. Both can double as travel crates, providing protection for the dog in the car. The size of the crate is another thing to consider. Puppies do not stay puppies forever—in fact, sometimes it seems as if they grow right before your eyes. A smaller crate may be fine for a very young Greyhound pup, but it will not do him much good for long! You are well advised to purchase the largest size crate available to accommodate a full-grown Greyhound properly.

The breeder has provided a den-like environment, complete with soft bedding material, for the Greyhound dam and her puppies.

BEDDING

A soft mat in the dog's crate will help the dog feel more at home, and you may also like to give him a small blanket. This will take the place of the leaves, twigs, etc., that the pup would use in the wild to make a den; the pup can make his own "burrow" in the crate. Although your pup is far removed from his den-making ancestors, the denning instinct is still a part of his genetic makeup. Second, until you take your pup home, he has been sleeping amid the warmth of his mother and litter-mates, and while a blanket is not the same as a warm, breathing body, it still provides heat and something with which to snuggle. You will want to wash your pup's bedding frequently in case he has an accident in his crate, and replace or remove any blanket or padding that becomes ragged and starts to fall apart.

TOYS

Toys are a must for dogs of all ages, especially for curious playful pups. Puppies are the "children" of the dog world, and what child does not love toys? Chew toys provide enjoyment to both dog and owner—your dog will enjoy playing with his favorite toys, while you will enjoy the fact that they distract him from your expensive shoes and leather sofa. Puppies love to chew; in fact, chewing is a physical need for pups as they are teething, and everything looks appetizing! The full range of your possessions—from old dish rag to Oriental carpet—are fair game in the eyes of a teething pup. Puppies are not all that discerning when it comes to finding something to literally "sink their teeth into"—every-thing tastes great!

Greyhound puppies are fairly aggres-sive chewers and only the strongest, most chew-resistant toys should be offered to them. Breeders advise owners to resist stuffed toys, because they can become de-stuffed in no time. The overly excited pup may ingest the stuff-ing, which could cause him to choke or become ill.

Similarly, squeaky toys are quite popular, but must be avoided for the Greyhound. Perhaps a squeaky toy can be used as an aid in training, but not for free play. If a pup "disem-bowels" one of these, the small plastic squeaker inside can be dangerous if swallowed. Monitor the condition of all your pup's toys carefully and get rid of any that have been chewed to the point of becoming dangerous.

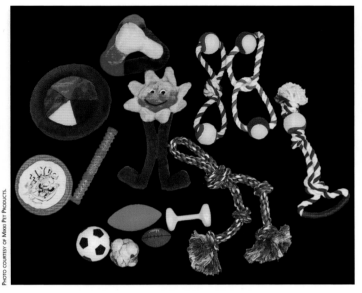

PHOTO COURTESY OF MIKKI PET PRODUCTS.

Your local pet shop should have a large variety of toys made especially for dogs. Never use toys made for humans; they are too weak for the wear and tear that a Greyhound puppy can inflict.

TOYS, TOYS, TOYS!

With a big variety of dog toys avail-able, and so many that look like they would be a lot of fun for a dog, be careful in your selection. It is amazing what a set of puppy teeth can do to an innocent-looking toy, so, obviously, safety is a major considera-tion. Be sure to choose the most durable products that you can find. Hard nylon bones and toys are a safe bet, and many of them are offered in different scents and flavors that will be sure to capture your dog's attention. It is always fun to play a game of fetch with your dog, and there are balls and flying discs that are specially made to withstand dog teeth.

Pet shops usually stock a wide assortment of leads. Greyhounds need lightweight yet sturdy nylon leads.

Be careful of natural bones, which have a tendency to splinter into sharp, dangerous pieces. Also be careful of rawhide, which can turn into pieces that are easy to swallow or into a mushy mess on your carpet.

LEAD

A nylon lead is probably the best option, as it is the most resistant to puppy teeth should your pup take a liking to chewing on his lead. Of course, this is a habit that should be nipped in the bud, but, if your pup likes to chew on his lead, he has a very slim chance of being able to chew through the strong nylon. Nylon leads are also lightweight, which is good for a young Greyhound who is just getting used to the idea of walking on a lead. For everyday walking and safety

purposes, the nylon lead is a good choice. As your pup grows up and gets used to walking on the lead, you may want to purchase a flexible lead. These leads allow you to extend the length to give the dog a broader area to explore or to shorten the length to keep the dog close to you. Be sure to purchase a flexible lead appropriate to your Greyhound's size, as these leads have weight limitations.

COLLAR

Your pup should get used to wearing a collar all the time since you will want to attach his ID tags to it. Plus, you have to attach the lead to something! A lightweight nylon collar is a good choice; make sure that it

FINANCIAL RESPONSIBILITY

Grooming tools, collars, leashes, a crate, a dog bed and, of course, toys will be expenses to you when you first obtain your pup, and the cost will continue throughout your dog's lifetime. If your puppy damages or destroys your possessions (as most puppies surely will!) or something belonging to a neighbor, you can calculate additional expense. There is also flea and pest control, which every dog owner faces more than once. You must be able to handle the financial responsibility of owning a dog.

CHOOSE AN APPROPRIATE COLLAR

The **BUCKLE COLLAR** is the standard collar used for everyday purposes. Be sure that you adjust the buckle on growing puppies. Check it every day. It can become too tight overnight! These collars can be made of leather or nylon. Attach your dog's identification tags to this collar.

The **CHOKE COLLAR** is designed for training. It is constructed of highly polished steel so that it slides easily through the stainless steel loop. The idea is that the dog controls the pressure around his neck and he will stop pulling if the collar becomes uncomfortable. It is used *only* during training and *never* left on a dog.

The **HALTER** is for a trained dog that has to be restrained to prevent running away, chasing a cat and the like. Considered the most humane of all collars, it is frequently used on smaller dogs on which collars are not comfortable.

A medium-weight
nylon collar and
lead are sufficient
for a well-trained
and disciplined
Greyhound.

fits snugly enough so that the pup cannot wriggle out of it, but is loose enough so that it will not be uncomfortably tight around the pup's neck. You should be able to fit a finger between the pup and the collar. It may take some time for your pup to get used to wearing the collar, but soon he will not even notice that it is there. Choke collars are made for training, but should only be used by a handler who knows how to use it properly.

FOOD AND WATER BOWLS
Your pup will need two bowls, one for food and one for water.

You may want two sets of bowls, one for inside and one for outside, depending on where the dog will be fed and where he will be spending most of his time. Stainless steel or sturdy plastic bowls are popular choices. Plastic bowls are more chewable. Dogs tend not to chew on the steel variety, which can be sterilized. It is important to buy sturdy bowls since anything is in danger of being chewed by puppy teeth and you do not want your dog to be constantly chewing apart his bowl. Also necessary are stands on which to elevate your Greyhound's bowls in order to prevent bloat.

Your local pet shop should carry a complete range of sturdy bowls for your dog's food and water.

Be a good citizen. Clean up after your dog. Your local pet shop will have helpful devices to make the task simpler.

PHOTO COURTESY OF MIKKI PET PRODUCTS.

CLEANING SUPPLIES

Until a pup is house-trained, you can expect to be doing a lot of cleaning. "Accidents" will occur, which is okay in the beginning because the puppy does not know any better. All you can do is be prepared to clean up any accidents. Old rags, towels, newspapers and a safe disinfectant are good to have on hand.

BEYOND THE BASICS

The items previously discussed are the bare necessities. You will find out what else you need as you go along—grooming supplies, baby gates to partition

DANGERS AT HOME

Scour your garage for potential doggie dangers. Remove weed killers, pesticides and antifreeze materials. Antifreeze is highly toxic and just a few drops can kill a puppy or an adult dog. The sweet taste attracts the animal, who will quickly consume it from the floor or pavement.

Thoroughly Greyhound-proof your house before bringing your new dog home. Never use cockroach or rodent poisons or plant fertilizers in any area accessible to the dog. Avoid the use of toilet cleaners. Most dogs are born with "toilet-bowl sonar" and will take a drink if the lid is left open. Also keep the trash secured and out of reach.

a room, etc. These things will vary depending on your situation, but it is important that right away you have everything you need to feed and make your Greyhound comfortable in his first few days at home.

GREYHOUND-PROOFING YOUR HOME

Aside from making sure that your Greyhound will be comfortable in your home, you also have to make sure that your home is safe for your Greyhound. This means taking precautions that your new charge will not get into anything he should not get into and that there is nothing within his reach that may harm him should he sniff it, chew it, inspect it, etc. This probably seems obvious since, while you are primarily concerned with your dog's safety, at the same time you do not want your belongings to be ruined. Adult and puppy Greyhounds are notorious snoops and thieves, and not much is out of this tall dog's reach.

Breakables should be placed out of reach if your dog is to have full run of the house. If he is to be limited to certain places within the house, keep any potentially dangerous items in the "off-limits" areas. An electrical cord can pose a danger should the dog decide to taste it—and who is going to convince a curious Greyhound that it would not make a great chew toy? Cords should be fastened tightly against the

NATURAL TOXINS
Examine your grass and landscaping before bringing your puppy home. Many varieties of plants have leaves, stems or flowers that are toxic if ingested, and you can depend on a curious puppy to investigate them. Ask your vet for information on poisonous plants or research them at your library, and make sure none are growing outside your home or kept in your home.

wall, out of the Greyhound's sight and reach. If your dog is going to spend time in a crate, make sure that there is nothing near his crate that he can reach if he sticks his curious nose or paws through the openings. Just as you would with a child, keep all household cleaners and chemicals where the dog cannot get to them.

It is also important to make sure that the outside of your home is safe. Of course, your Greyhound should never be unsupervised, but a pup or adult let loose in the yard will want to run and explore, and he should be granted that freedom. Do not let a fence give you a false sense of security; you would be surprised how crafty (and persistent) a dog can be in figuring out how to dig under and squeeze his way through holes, or to jump or climb over a

It is enjoyable to take the dam and puppies out for fun in the sun when the weather permits. The breeder provides early socialization opportunities such as this to encourage confidence, well-rounded personalities.

Fencing for the garden should be of sufficient height and sturdiness to ensure that the dog will not be able to escape.

shape and make repairs as needed; a very determined dog may return to the same spot to "work on it" until he is able to get through.

FIRST TRIP TO THE VET

You have selected your new Greyhound and your home and family are ready. Now all you have to do is collect your Greyhound from the breeder or adoption kennel and the fun begins, right? Well...not so fast. Something else you need to prepare is your dog's first trip to the veterinarian. Perhaps the breeder can recommend someone in the area who specializes in Greyhounds, or maybe you know some other Greyhound owners who can suggest a good vet. Either way, you should have an appointment arranged for your dog before you pick him up and visit the vet before taking him home.

The first visit will consist of an overall examination to make sure that the dog does not have

fence. Remember that an inadequate fence is no match for the Greyhound's sight-hound instincts, and perceived "prey" can have him off and running.

The remedy is to make the fence high enough so that it really is impossible for your dog to get over it (at least 6 feet should suffice), and well embedded into the ground. Be sure to repair or secure any gaps in the fence. Check the fence periodically to ensure that it is in good

IN DUE TIME

It will take at least two weeks for your puppy to become accustomed to his new surroundings. Give him lots of love, attention, handling, frequent opportunities to relieve himself, a diet he likes to eat and a place he can call his own.

any problems that are not apparent to you. For a new puppy, the vet will also set up a schedule for vaccinations; the breeder will inform you of which ones the pup has already received and the vet can continue from there. An adult may require vaccination boosters.

INTRODUCTION TO THE FAMILY

Everyone in the house will be excited about the dog's coming home and will want to pet him and play with him, but it is best to make the introductions low-key so as not to overwhelm the puppy. He is apprehensive already. It is the first time the pup has been separated from his mother and the breeder, and the ride to your home is likely the first time he has been in a car. An ex-racer may take some gentle socialization before meet-

ing too many new faces. The last thing you want to do is smother him, as this will only frighten him further. This is not to say that human contact is not extremely necessary at this stage, because this is the time when a connection between the dog and his human family is formed. Gentle petting and soothing words should help console him, as well as just putting him down and letting him explore on his own (under your watchful eye, of course).

The dog may approach the family members or may busy himself with exploring for a while. Gradually, each person should spend some time with the pup, one at a time, crouching down to get as close to the pup's level as possible while letting

Pretty as a picture both as a pup and adult! The Greyhound possesses an elegant beauty throughout all stages of life.

FEEDING TIPS
You will probably start feeding your pup the same food that he has been getting from the breeder; the breeder should give you a few days' supply to start you off. Although you should not give your pup too many treats, you will want to have puppy treats on hand for coaxing, training, rewards, etc. Be careful, though, as a small pup's calorie requirements are relatively low and a few treats can add up to almost a full day's worth of calories without the required nutrition.

Your Greyhound puppy is accustomed to the constant companionship of his mother and littermates, so he will need some time to get used to a new home and family.

him sniff their hands and petting him gently. He definitely needs human attention and he needs to be touched—this is how to form an immediate bond. Just remember that the pup is experiencing a lot of things for the first time, at the same time. There are new people, new noises, new smells and new things to investigate, so be gentle, be affectionate and be as comforting as you can be.

YOUR GREYHOUND'S FIRST NIGHT HOME

You have traveled home with your new charge safely in his crate. He's been to the vet for a thorough check-up; he's been weighed, his papers examined; perhaps he's even been vaccinated and wormed as well. He's met the family, and he's explored his area, his new bed, the yard and anywhere else he's been permitted. He's eaten his first meal at home and relieved himself in the proper place. He's heard lots of new sounds, smelled new friends and seen more of the outside world than ever before.

That was just the first day! He's worn out and is ready for bed...or so you think!

It's your Greyhound's first night home and you are ready to say "Good night." For a puppy,

When you bring a new puppy home, you take the place of his "pack leader." The pup has been getting affection and care from his mother from day one, and now it's up to you to take over that role.

this will be his first night sleeping alone; for an ex-racer, this my be his first time in a home environment. Either way, he's a bit scared, cold and lonely. Be reassuring to your new family member, but this is not the time to spoil him.

Puppies whine. They whine to let the others know where they are and hopefully to get company out of it. Place your pup in his new bed or crate in his room and close the door. Mercifully, he may fall asleep without a peep. When the inevitable occurs, ignore the whining: he is fine. Be strong and keep his interest in mind. Do not allow your heart to become guilty and visit the pup. He will fall asleep.

For a pup, many breeders recommend placing a piece of bedding from his former home in his new bed so that he recognizes the scent of his littermates. Others still advise placing a hot water bottle in his bed for warmth. This latter may be a good idea provided the pup does not attempt to suckle—he'll get good and wet and may not fall asleep so fast.

Your Greyhound's first night can be somewhat stressful for both the dog and his new family. Remember that you are setting the tone of nighttime at your house. Unless you want to play with your dog every evening at 10 p.m., midnight and 2 a.m., don't

TOXIC TREATS

Chocolate contains the chemical thebromine, which is poisonous to dogs, although "chocolates" especially made for dogs are safe (as they don't actually contain chocolate) but not recommended. Any item that encourages your dog to enjoy the taste of cocoa should be discouraged. You should also exercise caution when using mulch in your garden. This frequently contains cocoa hulls, and dogs have been known to die from eating the mulch. Onions are another "people food" poisonous to dogs.

initiate the habit. Your family will thank you, and soon so will your Greyhound!

PREVENTING PUPPY PROBLEMS

SOCIALIZATION

Now that you have done all of the preparatory work and have helped your pup get accustomed to his new home and family, it is about time for you to have some fun! Socializing your Greyhound gives you the opportunity to show off your new friend, and your dog gets to reap the benefits of being an intriguing creature that people will want to pet and, in general, think is absolutely fascinating!

Besides getting to know his new family, your Greyhound should be exposed to other people, animals and situations, but of course your pup must not come into close contact with dogs you don't know well until his course of injections is fully complete. Socialization will help him become well adjusted and less prone to being timid or fearful of the new things he will encounter.

Your pup's socialization began at the breeder's, but now it is your responsibility to continue it. The socialization he receives up until the age of 12 weeks is the most critical, as this is the time when he forms his impressions of the outside world. Be especially careful during the eight-to-ten-week-old period, also known as the fear period. The interaction he receives during this time should be gentle and reassuring. Lack of socialization can manifest itself in fear and aggression as the dog grows up. He needs lots of human contact, affection, handling and exposure to other animals. An ex-racer will not have been exposed to much of the outside world, so careful attention to his socialization is equally important.

Once your pup has received his necessary vaccinations, feel free to take him out and about (on his lead, of course). Walk him around the neighborhood, take him on your daily errands, let people pet him, let him meet other dogs and pets, etc. Puppies do not have to try to make friends; there will be no shortage of people who will want to introduce themselves. Just make sure that you carefully supervise each meeting. If the neighborhood children want to say hello, for example, that is great—children and pups most often make great companions. However, sometimes an excited child can unintentionally handle a pup too roughly, or an overzealous pup can playfully nip a little too hard. You want to make socialization experiences positive ones. What a pup learns during this very formative stage will affect his attitude toward future encounters. You want your dog to be comfortable around everyone. A pup that has a bad experience with a child may grow up to be a dog that is shy around or aggressive toward children.

PUP MEETS WORLD

Thorough socialization includes not only meeting new people but also being introduced to new experiences such as riding in the car, having his coat brushed, hearing the television, walking in a crowd—the list is endless. The more your pup experiences, and the more positive the experiences are, the less of a shock and the less frightening it will be for your pup to encounter new things.

CONSISTENCY IN TRAINING

Dogs, being pack animals, naturally need a leader, or else they try to establish dominance in their packs. When you bring a dog into your family, the choice of who becomes the leader and who becomes the "pack" is entirely up to you! Your pup's intuitive quest for dominance, coupled with the fact that it is nearly impossible to look at an adorable Greyhound pup with his sweet expression and "puppy-dog" eyes and not cave in, give the pup almost an unfair advantage in getting the upper hand! A pup will definitely test the waters to see what he can and cannot do. Do not give in to those pleading eyes—stand your ground when it comes to disciplining the pup and make sure that all family members do the same. It will only confuse the pup when Mother tells him to get off the sofa when he is used to sitting up there with Father to watch the nightly news. Avoid discrepancies by having all members of the household decide on the rules before the pup even comes home…and be consistent in enforcing them! Early training shapes the dog's personality, so you cannot be unclear in what you expect.

COMMON PUPPY PROBLEMS

The best way to prevent puppy problems is to be proactive in stopping an undesirable behavior as soon as it starts. The old saying "You can't teach an old dog new tricks" does not necessarily hold true, but it *is* true that it is much easier to discourage bad behavior in a young developing pup than to wait until the pup's bad behavior becomes the adult dog's bad habit. There are some problems that are especially prevalent in puppies as they develop.

NIPPING

As puppies start to teethe, they feel the need to sink their teeth into anything available…unfortunately that includes your fingers, arms, hair and toes. You may find this behavior cute for the first five seconds…until you feel just how sharp those puppy teeth are. This is something you want to discourage immediately and consistently with a firm "No!" (or whatever number of firm "Nos" it takes for him to understand that you

TRAINING HELP

Training your puppy takes much patience and can be frustrating at times, but you should see results from your efforts. If you have a puppy that seems untrainable, take him to a trainer or behaviorist. The dog may have a personality problem that requires the help of a professional, or perhaps you need help in learning how to train your dog.

mean business). Then replace your finger with an appropriate chew toy. While this behavior is merely annoying when the dog is young, it can become dangerous as your Greyhound's adult teeth grow in and his jaws develop, and he continues to

CHEWING TIPS

Chewing goes hand in hand with nipping in the sense that a teething puppy is always looking for a way to soothe his aching gums. In this case, instead of chewing on you, he may have taken a liking to your favorite shoe or something else that he should not be chewing. Again, realize that this is a normal canine behavior that does not need to be discouraged, only redirected. Your pup just needs to be taught what is acceptable to chew on and what is off-limits. Consistently tell him "No!" when you catch him chewing on something forbidden and give him a chew toy.

Conversely, praise him when you catch him chewing on something appropriate. In this way, you are discouraging the inappropriate behavior and reinforcing the desired behavior. The puppy's chewing should stop after his adult teeth have come in, but an adult dog continues to chew for various reasons—perhaps because he is bored, needs to relieve tension or just likes to chew. That is why it is important to redirect his chewing when he is still young.

think it is okay to nip at and nibble on his human friends. Your Greyhound does not mean any harm with a friendly nip, but he also does not know his own strength.

CRYING/WHINING

Your pup will often cry, whine, whimper, howl or make some type of commotion when he is left alone. This is basically his way of calling out for attention to make sure that you know he is there and that you have not forgotten about him. He feels insecure when he is left alone, when you are out of the house and he is in his crate or when you are in another part of the house and he cannot see you. The noise he is making is an expression of the anxiety he feels at being alone, so he needs to be taught that being alone is okay. You are not actually training the dog to stop making noise, you are training him to feel comfortable when he is alone and thus removing the need for him to make the noise.

This is where the crate with cozy bedding and a toy comes in handy. You want to know that he is safe when you are not there to supervise, and you know that he will be safe in his crate rather than roaming freely about the house. In order for the pup to stay in his crate

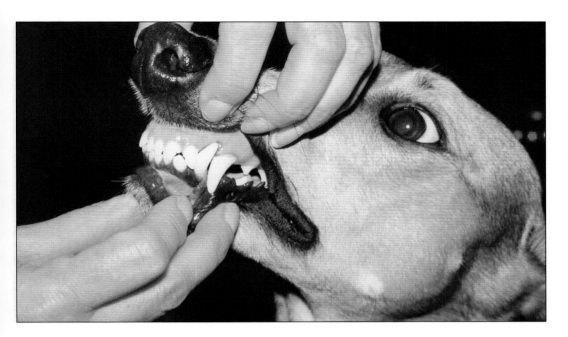

without making a fuss, he needs to be comfortable in his crate. On that note, it is extremely important that the crate is never used as a form of punishment, or the pup will develop a negative association with the crate.

Accustom the pup to the crate in short, gradually increasing time intervals in which you put him in the crate, maybe with a treat, and stay in the room with him. If he cries or makes a fuss, do not go to him, but stay in his sight. Gradually he will realize that staying in his crate is just fine without your help, and it will not be so traumatic for him

when you are not around. You may want to leave the radio on softly when you leave the house; the sound of human voices may be comforting.

NO PROBLEM!
The majority of problems that are commonly seen in young pups will disappear as your dog gets older. However, how you deal with problems when he is young will determine how he reacts to discipline as an adult dog. It is important to establish who is boss (ideally it will be you!) right away when you are first bonding with your dog. This bond will set the tone for the rest of your life together.

As your Greyhound grows, so do his teeth. Greyhounds, and all dogs for that matter, must chew in order to soothe their nerves and to maintain healthy gums and teeth.

DIETARY AND FEEDING CONSIDERATIONS

Today the choices of food for your Greyhound are many and varied. There are simply dozens of brands of food in all sorts of flavors and textures, ranging from puppy diets to those for seniors. There are even hypoallergenic and low-calorie diets available. Because your Greyhound's food has a bearing on coat, health and temperament, it is essential that the most suitable diet be selected for a Greyhound of his age. It is fair to say, however, that even experienced owners can be perplexed by the enormous range of foods available. Only understanding what is best for your dog will help you reach an informed decision.

Dog foods are produced in three basic types: dry, semi-moist and canned. Dry foods are useful for the cost-conscious, for overall they tend to be less expensive than semi-moist or canned. These contain the least fat and the most preservatives. In general, canned foods are made up of 60–70% water, while semi-moist ones often contain so much sugar that they are perhaps the least preferred by owners, even though their dogs seem to like them.

When selecting your dog's diet, three stages of development must be considered: the puppy stage, the adult stage and the senior stage.

PUPPY STAGE

Puppies instinctively want to suck milk from their mother's teats and a normal puppy will exhibit this behavior from just a few moments following birth. If puppies do not attempt to suckle within the first half-hour or so, they should be encouraged to do so by placing them on a nipple, having selected ones with plenty of milk. This early milk supply is important in providing colostrum to protect the puppies during the first eight to ten weeks of their lives. Although a mother's milk is much better

STORING DOG FOOD
You must store your dry dog food carefully. Open packages of dog food quickly lose their vitamin value, usually within 90 days of being opened. Mold spores and vermin could also contaminate the food.

than any milk formula, despite there being some excellent ones available, if the puppies do not feed, the breeder will have to feed them himself. For those with less experience, advice from a veterinarian is important so that not only the right quantity of milk is fed but also that of correct quality, fed at suitably frequent intervals, usually every two hours during the first few days of life.

Puppies should be allowed to

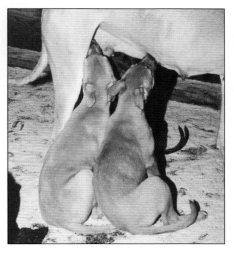

Puppies instinctively suck milk from their mother. Many vets recommend that pups be allowed to suckle for at least six weeks and be fully weaned by seven to eight weeks.

FOOD PREFERENCE

Selecting the best dry dog food is difficult. There is no majority consensus among veterinary scientists as to the value of nutrient analysis (protein, fat, fiber, moisture, ash, cholesterol, minerals, etc.). All agree that feeding trials are what matter most, but you also have to consider the individual dog. The dog's weight, age and activity level, and what pleases his taste, all must be considered. It is probably best to take the advice of your veterinarian. Every dog has individual dietary requirements, and should be fed accordingly.

If your dog is fed a good dry food, he does not require supplements of meat or vegetables. Dogs do appreciate a little variety in their diets, so you may choose to stay with the same brand but vary the flavor. Alternatively, you may wish to add a little flavored stock to give a difference to the taste.

nurse from their mothers for about the first six weeks, although from the third or fourth week the breeder will begin to introduce small portions of suitable solid food. Most breeders like to introduce alternate milk and meat meals initially, building up to weaning time.

By the time the puppies are seven or a maximum of eight weeks old, they should be fully weaned and fed solely on a proprietary puppy food. Selection of the most suitable, best-quality diet at this time is essential, for a puppy's fastest growth rate is during the first year of life. You do not want to overfeed a young Greyhound, as this can create orthopedic problems later in life due to the stress on the joints and bones. Your vet and/or breeder will be able to offer advice in this regard.

Puppy and junior diets should be well balanced for the needs of your dog, so that, except in certain circumstances, additional vitamins, minerals and proteins will not be required.

ADULT DIETS

A dog is considered an adult when he has stopped growing, so in general the diet of a Greyhound can be changed to an adult one at about 10–12 months of age. Again you should rely upon your veterinarian or breeder to recommend an acceptable maintenance diet. Major dog-food manufacturers specialize in this type of food, and it is just necessary for you to select the one best suited to your dog's needs. Active dogs may have different requirements than more sedate dogs. Although lean in build, the Greyhound does have a hearty appetite!

SENIOR DIETS

As dogs get older, their metabolism changes. The older dog usually exercises less, moves more slowly and sleeps more. This change in lifestyle and physiological performance requires a change in diet. Since these changes take place slowly, they might not be recognizable. What is easily recognizable is weight gain. By continuing to feed your dog an adult-maintenance diet when he is slowing down metabolically, your dog will gain weight. Obesity in an older dog compounds the health problems that already accompany old age.

As your dog gets older, few of his organs function up to par. The kidneys slow down and the intestines become less efficient. These age-related factors are best handled with a change in diet and a change in feeding schedule to give smaller portions that are more easily digested.

There is no single best diet for every older dog. While many dogs do well on light or senior diets, other dogs do better on special premium diets such as lamb and rice. Be sensitive to your senior Greyhound's diet and this will help control other problems that may arise with your old friend.

GRAIN-BASED DIETS

Some less expensive dog foods are based on grains and other plant proteins. While these products may appear to be attractively priced, many breeders prefer a diet based on animal proteins and believe that they are more conducive to your dog's health. Many grain-based diets rely on soy protein, which may cause flatulence (passing gas).

There are many cases, however, when your dog might require a special diet. These special requirements should only be recommended by your veterinarian.

TEST FOR PROPER DIET

A good test for proper diet is the color, odor and firmness of your dog's stool. A healthy dog usually produces three semi-hard stools per day. The stools should have no unpleasant odor. They should be the same color from excretion to excretion.

WATER

Just as your dog needs proper nutrition from his food, water is an essential "nutrient" as well. Water keeps the dog's body properly hydrated and promotes normal function of the body's systems. During housebreaking, it is necessary to keep an eye on how much water your Greyhound pup is drinking, but, once he is reliably trained, he should have

Puppy diets are different than adult diets. Young pups usually eat meat meals as part of the weaning process.

Your Greyhound's food and water bowls should be placed on an elevated surface. The dog should not have to strain and bend to the floor to eat; reaching and craning his neck introduces air, a major contributor to bloat.

access to clean fresh water at all times. Make sure that the dog's water bowl is clean and elevated, and change the water often, making sure that a fresh supply of water is available for your dog. Some breeders advise withholding water during mealtimes, thereby lessening the possibility of bloat.

EXERCISE

The Greyhound requires more exercise than most other breeds of dog. The combination of the dog's athletic nature, long limbs and inborn desire to run makes this a high-maintenance breed to keep in optimum physical shape. A sedentary lifestyle is as harmful to

a dog as it is to a person. Long walks, play sessions in the fenced yard and letting the dog run free in the yard or other secure area under your supervision are daily forms of exercise for your Greyhound. For those who are more ambitious, you will find that your Greyhound also enjoys an occasional hike or even a swim!

Some tips to remember: First, restrict exercise for at least an hour before and after meals. Second, bear in mind that an overweight dog should never be suddenly over-exercised; instead, he should be encouraged to increase exercise slowly. Third, remember that not only is exercise

A Worthy Investment

Veterinary studies have proven that a balanced high-quality diet pays off in your dog's coat quality, behavior and activity level. Invest in premium brands for the maximum payoff with your dog.

When your Greyhound puppy is hungry, he'll be sure to find a creative way to let you know!

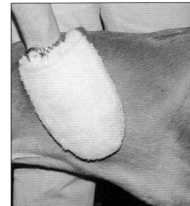

essential to keep the dog's body fit, it is essential to his mental well-being. A bored dog will find something to do, which often manifests itself in some type of destructive behavior. In this sense, it is just as essential for the owner's mental well-being!

GROOMING

BRUSHING

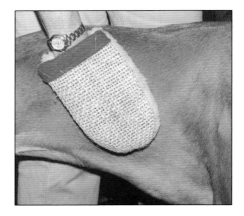

Types of grooming gloves. Top: Showing the sheepskin side of the "cactus," i.e., using the cactus cloth side on the dog. Center: Showing the cactus cloth side of the "cactus," i.e., using the sheepskin side on the dog. Bottom: Showing the bristles on a hound glove.

A natural bristle brush or a hound glove can be used for regular routine brushing. Daily brushing is effective for removing dead hair and stimulating the dog's natural oils to add shine and a healthy look to the coat. Although the Greyhound's coat is short and close, it does require a regular once-over, once or twice weekly, to keep it looking its shiny best. Regular grooming sessions are also a good way to spend time with your dog. Many dogs grow to like the feel of being brushed and will enjoy the routine.

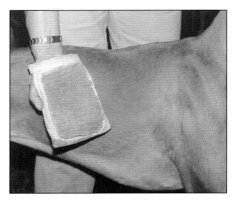

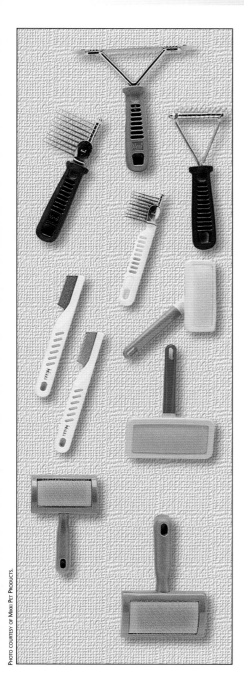

BATHING

Dogs do not need to be bathed as often as humans, but bathing as needed is important for healthy skin and a clean, shiny coat. Again, like most anything, if you accustom your pup to being bathed as a puppy, it will be second nature by the time he grows up. You want your dog to be at ease in the bath or else it could end up a wet, soapy, messy ordeal for both of you!

Brush your Greyhound thoroughly before wetting his coat. Make certain that your dog has a good non-slip surface to stand on. Begin by wetting the dog's coat. A shower or hose attachment is necessary for thoroughly wetting

There is not much required for grooming a Greyhound, but your pet shop will have many brushes from which you can make a selection. Follow your vet's or breeder's advice about which grooming supplies to use.

GROOMING EQUIPMENT

How much grooming equipment you purchase will depend on how much grooming you are going to do. Here are some basics:

- Natural bristle brush
- Hound glove
- Flea comb
- Rubber mat
- Dog shampoo
- Spray hose attachment
- Towels
- Ear cleaner
- Cotton balls
- Nail clippers
- Dental-care products

and rinsing the coat. Check the water temperature to make sure that it is neither too hot nor too cold for the dog.

Next, apply shampoo to the dog's coat and work it into a good lather. You should purchase a shampoo that is made for dogs. Do not use a product made for human hair. Wash the head last; you do not want shampoo to drip into the dog's eyes while you are washing the rest of his body. Work the shampoo all the way down to the skin. You can use this opportunity to check the skin for any bumps, bites or other abnormalities. Do not neglect any area of the body— get all of the hard-to-reach places.

Once the dog has been thoroughly shampooed, he requires an equally thorough rinsing. Shampoo left in the coat can be irritating to the skin. Protect his eyes from the shampoo by shielding them with your hand and directing the flow of water in the opposite direction. You should also avoid getting water in the ear canal. Be prepared for your dog to shake out his coat—you might want to stand back, but make sure you have a hold on the dog to keep him from running through the house.

EAR CLEANING

The ears should be kept clean and any excess hair inside the ear should be carefully plucked out. Ears can be cleaned with soft cotton and an ear-cleaning powder or liquid made especially for dogs. Be on the lookout for any signs of infection or ear-mite infestation. If your Greyhound has been shaking his head or scratching at his ears frequently, this usually indicates a problem. If his ears have an unusual odor, this is a sure sign of mite infestation or infection, and a signal to have his ears checked by the veterinarian.

NAIL CLIPPING

Your Greyhound should be accustomed to having his nails trimmed at an early age, since it will be part of your maintenance routine throughout his life. Not only does it look nicer, but long nails can scratch someone unintentionally.

BATHING BEAUTY

Once you are sure that the dog is thoroughly rinsed, squeeze the excess water out of his coat with your hand and dry him with a heavy towel. You may choose to use a blow dryer, on low heat, on his coat or just let it dry naturally. In cold weather, never allow your dog outside with a wet coat.

There are "dry bath" products on the market, which are sprays and powders intended for spot cleaning that can be used between regular baths if necessary. They are not substitutes for regular baths, but they are easy to use for touch-ups as they do not require rinsing.

Also, a long nail has a better chance of ripping and bleeding, or of causing the feet to spread. A good rule of thumb is that if you can hear your dog's nails' clicking on the floor when he walks, his nails are too long.

Before you start cutting, make sure you can identify the "quick" in each nail. The quick is a blood vessel that runs through the center of each nail and grows rather close to the end. It will bleed if accidentally cut, which will be quite painful for the dog as it contains nerve endings. Keep some type of clotting agent on hand, such as a styptic pencil or styptic powder (the type used for shaving). This will stop the bleeding quickly when applied to the end of the cut nail. Do not panic if this happens, just stop the bleeding and talk soothingly to your dog. Once he has calmed down, move on to the next nail. It is better to clip a little at a time,

SOAP IT UP
The use of human soap products like shampoo, bubble bath and hand soap can be damaging to a dog's coat and skin. Human products are too strong; they remove the protective oils coating the dog's hair and skin that make him water-resistant. Use only shampoo made especially for dogs. You may like to use a medicated shampoo, which will help to keep external parasites at bay.

particularly with dark-nailed dogs.

Hold your pup steady as you begin trimming his nails; you do not want him to make any sudden movements or run away. Talk to him soothingly and stroke him as you clip. Holding his foot in your hand, simply take off the end of each nail in one quick clip. You can purchase nail clippers that are specially made for dogs; you can

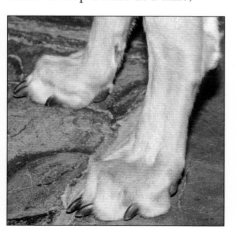

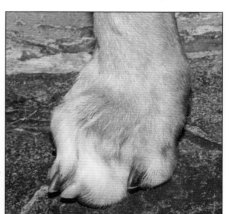

Left: Greyhound's front feet. Right: Greyhound's back foot. A proper Greyhound foot is compact and well-knuckled, and maintained in neat condition with trimmed nails.

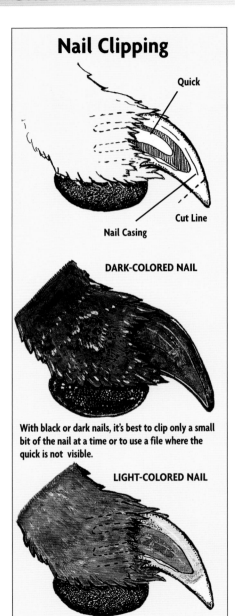

Nail Clipping

Quick

Cut Line

Nail Casing

DARK-COLORED NAIL

With black or dark nails, it's best to clip only a small bit of the nail at a time or to use a file where the quick is not visible.

LIGHT-COLORED NAIL

In light-colored nails, clipping is much simpler because you can see the vein (or quick) that grows inside the casing.

probably find them wherever you buy pet supplies.

TRAVELING WITH YOUR DOG

CAR TRAVEL

You should accustom your Greyhound to riding in a car at an early age. You may or may not take him in the car often, but at the very least he will need to go to the vet and you do not want these trips to be traumatic for the dog or troublesome for you. The safest way for a dog to ride in the car is in his crate. If he uses a crate in the house, you can use the same crate for travel. Of course, the average car is not large enough to accommodate the Greyhound's crate, so a sport utility vehicle or van will be on the Greyhound owner's wish list.

Put the pup in the crate and see how he reacts. If he seems uneasy, you can have a passenger hold him on his lap while you drive. Another option is a specially made safety harness for

ON-LEAD ONLY

When traveling, never let your dog off-lead in a strange area. Your dog could run away out of fear, decide to chase a passing squirrel or cat or simply want to stretch his legs without restriction—if any of these happen, you might never see your canine friend again.

dogs, which straps the dog in much like a seat belt. Do not let the dog roam loose in the vehicle—this is very dangerous! If you should stop short, your dog can be thrown and injured. If the dog starts climbing on you and pestering you while you are driving, you will not be able to concentrate on the road. It is an unsafe situation for everyone—human and canine.

For long trips, bring along water for the dog and make stops to let him relieve himself. Take with you whatever you need to clean up after him, including some paper towels and perhaps some old rags for use should he have a potty accident in the car or suffer from motion sickness.

AIR TRAVEL

Contact your chosen airline before proceeding with your travel plans that include your Greyhound. The dog will be required to travel in a fiberglass crate and you should always check in advance with the

Never travel with your Greyhound unrestrained in the car. Use a crate for your safety, the dog's safety and the safety of your passengers.

airline regarding specific requirements for the crate, as well as any travel restrictions and health certificates. To help put the dog at ease, give him one of his favorite toys in the crate. Do not feed the dog for several hours before the trip in order to minimize his need to relieve himself. Your airline may ask you for documentation as to when the dog was last fed. In any case, a light meal is best.

Make sure your dog is properly identified and that your contact information appears on his ID tags and on his crate. Animals travel in a different area of the plane than human passengers, so every rule must be strictly followed so as to prevent the risk of getting separated from your dog. Be sure you take the time to talk to the airline representative at the gate so that the crew understands that they have "precious cargo" on board. If you get an apathetic, nonchalant response from the attendant, you might be well advised to not board the plane. Greyhounds (as well as

HOT-WEATHER HINT

Never leave your dog alone in the car. In hot weather, your dog can die from the high temperature inside a closed vehicle; even a car parked in the shade can heat up very quickly. Leaving the window open is dangerous as well since the dog can hurt himself trying to get out.

other dogs) can become overheated in their crates in a short amount of time, and heat exhaustion can be deadly. A few years ago, a well-known American show Greyhound expired while a plane was delayed on the runway. Despite the owner's frantic attempts to alert the crew that her dog was in the cargo department, the unresponsive crew did not get to the dog in time. The moral of this sad tale is for you to be actively concerned whenever boarding your dog on a flight. Most times, there is nothing to worry about, but don't let your dog become an unfortunate exception.

VACATIONS AND BOARDING

So you want to take a family vacation—and you want to include *all* members of the family. You would probably make arrangements for accommodations ahead of time anyway, but this is especially important when traveling with a dog. You do not want to make an overnight stop at the only place around for miles and find out that they do not allow dogs. Also, you do not want to reserve a place for your family without confirming that you are traveling with a dog because, if it is against their policy, you may not have a place to stay.

Alternatively, if you are traveling and choose not to bring your Greyhound, you will have to make arrangements for him while you are away. Some options are to take him to a neighbor's house to stay while you are gone, to have a trusted friend stop by often or stay at your house or to bring your dog to a reputable boarding kennel. If you choose to board him at a kennel, you should visit in advance to see the facilities, how clean they are and where the dogs are kept. Talk to some of the employees and see how they treat the dogs—do they spend time with the dogs, play with them, exercise them, etc.? Also find out the kennel's policy on vaccinations and what they require. This is for all of the dogs' safety, since when dogs are kept together,

there is a greater risk of diseases being passed from dog to dog.

IDENTIFICATION

Your Greyhound is your valued companion and friend. That is why you always keep a close eye on him and you have made sure that he cannot escape from the yard or wriggle out of his collar and run away from you. However, accidents can happen and there may come a time when your dog unexpectedly gets separated from you. If this unfortunate event should occur, the first thing on your mind will be finding him. Proper identification, including an ID tag and possibly a tattoo and/or a microchip, will increase the chances of his being returned to you safely.

IDENTIFICATION OPTIONS

As puppies become more and more expensive, especially those puppies of high quality for showing and/or breeding, they have a greater chance of being stolen. The usual collar dog tag is, of course, easily removed. But there are two more permanent techniques that have become widely used for identification purposes.

The puppy microchip implantation involves the injection of a small microchip, about the size of a corn kernel, under the skin of the dog. If your dog shows up at a clinic or shelter, or is offered for resale under less-than-savory circumstances, he can be positively identified by the microchip. The microchip is scanned, and a registry quickly identifies you as the owner.

Tattooing is done on various parts of the dog, from his belly to his ears. The number tattooed can be your telephone number, your dog's registration number or any other number that you can easily memorize. When professional dog thieves see a tattooed dog, they usually lose interest. For the safety of our dogs, no laboratory facility or dog broker will accept a tattooed dog as stock.

Discuss microchipping and tattooing with your veterinarian and breeder. Some vets perform these services on their own premises for a reasonable fee. To ensure that your dog's identification is effective, be certain that the dog is then properly registered with a legitimate national database.

If you are going to board your Greyhound, the kennel must be large enough to afford the dog ample space to exercise and move about.

TRAINING YOUR

GREYHOUND

Living with an untrained dog is a lot like owning a piano that you do not know how to play—it is a nice object to look at, but it does not do much more than that to bring you pleasure. Now try taking piano lessons, and suddenly the piano comes alive and brings forth magical sounds and rhythms that set your heart singing and your body swaying.

The same is true with your Greyhound. Any dog is a big responsibility and, if not trained sensibly, may develop unacceptable behavior that annoys you or could even cause family friction.

To train your Greyhound, you may like to enroll in an obedience

class. Teach him good manners as you learn how and why he behaves the way he does. Find out how to communicate with your dog and how to recognize and understand his communications with you. Suddenly the dog takes on a new role in your life—he is smart, interesting, well behaved and fun to be with. He demonstrates his bond of devotion to you daily. In other words, your Greyhound does wonders for your ego because he constantly reminds you that you are not only his leader, you are his hero!

Those involved with teaching dog obedience and counseling owners about their dogs' behavior have discovered some interesting facts about dog ownership. For example, training dogs when they are puppies results in the highest rate of success in developing well-mannered and well-adjusted adult dogs. Training an older dog, from six months to six years of age, can produce almost equal results, providing that the owner accepts the dog's slower rate of learning capability and is willing to work patiently to help the dog succeed at developing to his fullest potential. Unfortunately, many owners

REAP THE REWARDS

If you start with a normal, healthy dog and give him time, patience and some carefully executed lessons, you will reap the rewards of that training for the life of the dog. And what a life it will be! The two of you will find immeasurable pleasure in the companionship you have built together with love, respect and understanding.

of untrained adult dogs lack the patience factor, so they do not persist until their dogs are successful at learning particular behaviors.

Training a puppy aged 10 to 16 weeks (20 weeks at the most) is like working with a dry sponge in a pool of water. The pup soaks up whatever you show him and constantly looks for more things to do and learn. At this early age, his body is not yet producing hormones, and therein lies the reason for such a high rate of success. Without hormones, he is focused on his owners and not particularly interested in investigating other places, dogs, people, etc. You are his leader: his provider of food, water, shelter and security. He latches onto you and wants to stay close. He will usually follow you from room to room, will not let you out of his sight when you are outdoors with him and will respond in like

The intelligent, alert Greyhound makes an exemplary student, provided his owners approach his education with patience and consistency. Although not as eager as some of the retriever or shepherding breeds, Greyhounds can be trained to obey dozens of commands.

manner to the people and animals you encounter. If you greet a friend warmly, he will be happy to greet the person as well. If, however, you are hesitant or anxious about the approach of a stranger, he will respond accordingly to you.

Once the puppy begins to produce hormones, his natural curiosity emerges and he begins to investigate the world around him. It is at this time when you may notice that the untrained dog begins to wander away from you and even ignore your commands to stay close. When this behavior becomes a problem, you have two

PARENTAL GUIDANCE

Training a dog is a life experience. Many parents admit that much of what they know about raising children they learned from caring for their dogs. Dogs respond to love, fairness and guidance, just as children do. Become a good dog owner and you may become an even better parent.

choices: get rid of the dog or train him. It is strongly urged that you choose the latter option.

There will usually be classes within a reasonable distance from your home, but you can also do a lot to train your dog yourself. Sometimes there are classes available, but the tuition is too costly. Whatever the circumstances, the solution to training your Greyhound without formal obedience classes lies within the pages of this book.

This chapter is devoted to helping you train your Greyhound at home. If the recommended procedures are followed faithfully, you may expect positive results that will prove rewarding to both you and your dog.

Whether your new charge is a puppy or a mature adult, the methods of teaching and the techniques we use in training basic behaviors are the same. After all,

no dog, whether puppy or adult, likes harsh or inhumane methods. All creatures, however, respond favorably to gentle motivational methods and sincere praise and encouragement. Now let us get started.

HOUSEBREAKING

You can train a puppy to relieve himself wherever you choose, but this must be somewhere suitable. You should bear in mind from the outset that when your puppy is old enough to go out in public places, any canine droppings must be removed at once. You will always have to carry with you a small plastic bag or "poop-scoop."

Outdoor training includes such surfaces as grass, dirt and cement. Indoor training usually means training your dog to newspaper, although that's not the best option with a large dog like the Greyhound. When deciding on the surface and location that you will want your Greyhound to use, be sure it is going to be permanent. Training your dog to grass and then changing your mind two months later is extremely difficult for both dog and owner.

Next, choose the command you will use each and every time you want your puppy to void. "Go hurry up" and "Let's go" are examples of commands commonly used by dog owners.

Get in the habit of giving the

THINK BEFORE YOU BARK
Dogs are sensitive to their masters' moods and emotions. Use your voice wisely when communicating with your dog. Never raise your voice at your dog unless you are trying to correct him. "Barking" at your dog can become as meaningless as "dogspeak" is to you.

puppy your chosen relief command before you take him out. That way, when he becomes an adult, you will be able to determine if he wants to go out when you ask him. A confirmation will be signs of interest, such as wagging his tail, watching you intently, going to the door, etc.

PUPPY'S NEEDS

Your puppy needs to relieve himself after play periods, after each meal, after he has been sleeping and any time he indicates that he is looking for a place to urinate or defecate. The urinary and intestinal tract muscles of very young puppies are not fully developed. Therefore, like human babies, puppies need to relieve themselves frequently.

Take your puppy out often—every hour for an eight-week-old, for example, and always immediately after sleeping and eating.

Your puppy will return to the same area to relieve himself, so make sure the area is one that you have chosen for him.

The older the puppy, the less often he will need to relieve himself. Finally, as a mature healthy adult, he will require only three to five relief trips per day.

HOUSING

Since the types of housing and control you provide for your puppy have a direct relationship on the success of house-training, we consider the various aspects of both before we begin training.

Taking a new puppy home and turning him loose in your house can be compared to turning a child loose in a gymnasium and telling the child that the place is

Humans must adopt clean habits, too—pick up after your dog every time.

MEALTIME

Mealtime should be a peaceful time for your puppy. Do not put his food and water bowls in a high-traffic area in the house. For example, give him his own little corner of the kitchen where he can eat undisturbed and where he will not be underfoot. Do not allow small children or other family members to disturb the pup when he is eating.

What you feed your Greyhound is very important. The dog does not need variety; he does need a complete and balanced diet. Get your vet's recommendations when it comes to your Greyhound's diet.

all his! The sheer enormity of the place would be too much for him to handle.

Instead, offer the puppy clearly defined areas where he can play, sleep, eat and live. A room of the house where the family gathers is the most obvious choice. Puppies are social animals and need to feel a part of the pack right from the start. Hearing your voice, watching you while you are doing things and smelling you nearby are all positive reinforcers that he is now a member of your pack. Usually a family room, the kitchen or a nearby adjoining breakfast area is ideal for providing safety and security for both puppy and owner.

Within that room, there should be a smaller area that the puppy can call his own. An alcove, a wire or fiberglass dog crate or a gated corner from which he can view the activities of his new family will be fine. The size of the area or crate is the key factor here. The area must be large enough for the puppy to lie down and stretch out as well as stand up without rubbing his head on the top, yet small enough so that

HONOR AND OBEY

Dogs are the most honorable animals in existence. They consider another species (humans) as their own. They interface with you. You are their leader. Puppies perceive children to be on their level; their actions around small children are different from their behavior around their adult masters.

CANINE DEVELOPMENT SCHEDULE

It is important to understand how and at what age a puppy develops into adulthood. If you are a puppy owner, consult the following Canine Development Schedule to determine the stage of development your puppy is currently experiencing. This knowledge will help you as you work with the puppy in the weeks and months ahead.

Period	Age	Characteristics
FIRST TO THIRD	**BIRTH TO SEVEN WEEKS**	Puppy needs food, sleep and warmth, and responds to simple and gentle touching. Needs mother for security and disciplining. Needs littermates for learning and interacting with other dogs. Pup learns to function within a pack and learns pack order of dominance. Begin socializing pup with adults and children for short periods. Pup begins to become aware of his environment.
FOURTH	**EIGHT TO TWELVE WEEKS**	Brain is fully developed. Pup needs socializing with outside world. Remove from mother and littermates. Needs to change from canine pack to human pack. Human dominance necessary. Fear period occurs between 8 and 12 weeks. Avoid fright and pain.
FIFTH	**THIRTEEN TO SIXTEEN WEEKS**	Training and formal obedience should begin. Less association with other dogs, more with people, places, situations. Period will pass easily if you remember this is pup's change-to-adolescence time. Be firm and fair. Flight instinct prominent. Permissiveness and over-disciplining can do permanent damage. Praise for good behavior.
JUVENILE	**FOUR TO EIGHT MONTHS**	Another fear period about 7 to 8 months of age. It passes quickly, but be cautious of fright and pain. Sexual maturity reached. Dominant traits established. Dog should understand sit, down, come and stay by now.

NOTE: THESE ARE APPROXIMATE TIME FRAMES. ALLOW FOR INDIVIDUAL DIFFERENCES IN PUPPIES.

he cannot relieve himself at one end and sleep at the other without coming into contact with his droppings. Dogs are, by nature, clean animals and will not remain close to their relief areas unless forced to do so. In those cases, they then become dirty dogs and usually remain that way for life.

The designated area should be lined with clean bedding and a toy. Water must always be available, in a non-spill container, although you'll want to monitor your pup's water intake during housebreaking so you'll know when he needs "to go."

CONTROL

By *control*, we mean helping the puppy to create a lifestyle pattern that will be compatible to that of his human pack (*you!*). Just as we guide little children to learn our way of life, we must show the puppy when it is time to play, eat, sleep, exercise and even entertain himself.

Your puppy should always sleep in his crate. He should also learn that, during times of household confusion and excessive

> **PAPER CAPER**
> Never line your pup's sleeping area with newspaper. Puppy litters are usually raised on newspaper and, once in your home, the puppy will immediately associate newspaper with voiding. Never put newspaper on any floor while house-training, as this will only confuse the puppy. Finally, restrict water intake after evening meals. Offer a few licks at a time— never let a Greyhound of any age gulp water after meals.

human activity such as at breakfast when family members are preparing for the day, he can play by himself in relative safety and comfort in his designated area. Each time you leave the puppy alone, he should understand exactly where he is to stay. Puppies are chewers. They cannot tell the difference between things like lamp cords, television wires, shoes, table legs, etc. Chewing into a television wire, for example, can be fatal to the puppy, while a shorted wire can start a fire in the house.

If the puppy chews on the arm of the chair when he is alone, you will probably discipline him angrily when you get home. Thus, he makes the association that your coming home means he is going to be punished. (He will not remem-

An open crate is fine for inside your home. For puppies, however, never put the water bowl inside the crate. This invites accidents when the puppy is crated.

> ### ATTENTION!
> Your dog is actually training you at the same time you are training him. Dogs do things to get attention. They usually repeat whatever succeeds in getting your attention.

ber chewing the chair and is incapable of making the association of the discipline with his naughty deed.) Accustoming the pup to his crate keeps him from engaging in dangerous and destructive behaviors when you cannot supervise.

Further, times of excitement, such as family parties, visits from friends, etc., can be fun for the puppy, providing he can view the activities from the security of his designated area. He is not underfoot and he is not being fed all sorts of tidbits that will probably cause him stomach distress, yet he still feels a part of the fun.

SCHEDULE

A puppy should be taken to his relief area each time he is released from his designated area, after meals, after play sessions, when he first awakens in the morning (at age eight weeks, this can mean 5 a.m.!). The puppy will indicate that he's ready "to go" by circling or sniffing busily—do not misinterpret these signs. For a puppy less than ten weeks of age, a routine of taking him out every

hour is necessary. As the puppy grows, he will be able to wait for longer periods of time.

Keep trips to his relief area short. Stay no more than five or six minutes and then return to the house. If he goes during that time, praise him lavishly and take him indoors immediately. If he does not, but he has an accident when you go back indoors, pick him up immediately, say "No! No!" and return to his relief area. Wait a few minutes, then return to the house again. Never hit a puppy or put his face in urine or excrement when he has an accident!

Once indoors, put the puppy in his crate until you have had time to clean up his accident. Then release him to the family area and watch him more closely than before. Chances are, his accident was a result of your not picking up his signal or waiting too long before offering him the opportunity to relieve himself.

A puppy should be taken to his relief area very frequently. Usually a young puppy will need to relieve himself every hour when he is awake.

HOW MANY TIMES A DAY?

AGE	RELIEF TRIPS
To 14 weeks	10
14–22 weeks	8
22–32 weeks	6
Adulthood	4
(dog stops growing)	

These are estimates, of course, but they are a guide to the *minimum* number of opportunities a dog should have each day to relieve himself.

A crated puppy will usually urinate as soon as he is allowed freedom to visit his relief site. Crate training is an extremely successful housebreaking method.

Never hold a grudge against the puppy for accidents.

Let the puppy learn that going outdoors means it is time to relieve himself, not play. Once trained, he will be able to play indoors and out and still differentiate between the times for play versus the times for relief.

Help your pup develop regular hours for naps, being alone, playing by himself and just resting, all in his crate. Encourage him to entertain himself while you are busy with your activities. Let him learn that having you near is comforting, but it is not your main purpose in life to provide him with undivided attention. Each time you put your puppy in his own area, use the same command, whatever suits best. Soon, he will run to his crate or special area when he hears you say those words.

Crate training provides safety for you, the puppy and the home. It also provides the puppy with a feeling of security, and that helps the puppy achieve self-confidence and clean habits. Remember that one of the primary ingredients in house-training your puppy is control. Regardless of your lifestyle, there will always be occasions when you will need to have a place where your dog can stay and be happy and safe. Crate training is the answer for now and in the future.

In conclusion, a few key elements are really all you need for a successful house-training method—consistency, frequency, praise, control and supervision. By following these procedures with a normal, healthy puppy, you and the puppy will soon be past the stage of "accidents" and ready to move on to a clean and rewarding life together.

ROLES OF DISCIPLINE, REWARD AND PUNISHMENT

Discipline, training one to act in accordance with rules, brings order to life. It is as simple as that. Without discipline, particularly in a group society, chaos reigns supreme and the group will eventually perish. Humans and canines are social animals and need some form of discipline in order to function effectively. They must procure food, protect their home base and reproduce to keep the species going.

If there were no discipline in the lives of social animals, they would eventually die from starva-

THE SUCCESS METHOD

Success that comes by luck is usually short-lived. Success that comes by well-thought-out proven methods is often more easily achieved and permanent. This is the Success Method. It is designed to give you, the puppy owner, a simple yet proven way to help your puppy develop clean living habits and a feeling of security in his new environment.

6 Steps to Successful Crate Training

1 Tell the puppy "Crate time!" and place him in the crate with a small treat (a piece of cheese or half of a biscuit). Let him stay in the crate for five minutes while you are in the same room. Then release him and praise lavishly. Never release him when he is fussing. Wait until he is quiet before you let him out.

2 Repeat Step 1 several times a day.

3 The next day, place the puppy in the crate as before. Let him stay there for ten minutes. Do this several times.

4 Continue building time in five-minute increments until the puppy stays in his crate for 30 minutes with you in the room. Always take him to his relief area after prolonged periods in his crate.

5 Now go back to Step 1 and let the puppy stay in his crate for five minutes, this time while you are out of the room.

6 Once again, build crate time in five-minute increments with you out of the room. When the puppy will stay willingly in his crate (he may even fall asleep!) for 30 minutes with you out of the room, he will be ready to stay in it for several hours at a time.

Greyhounds are very inquisitive dogs, with the size and speed to get into and reach almost anything. Keep this in mind and keep any breakable or potentially harmful items safely away from your dog.

tion and/or predation by other stronger animals. In the case of domestic canines, dogs need discipline in their lives in order to understand how their pack (you

and other family members) functions and how they must act in order to survive.

A large humane society in a highly populated area recently surveyed dog owners regarding their satisfaction with their relationships with their dogs. People who had trained their dogs were 75% more satisfied with their pets than those who had never trained their dogs.

Dr. Edward Thorndike, a famous psychologist, established *Thorndike's Theory of Learning*, which states that a behavior that results in a pleasant event tends to be repeated. Conversely, a behavior that results in an unpleasant event tends not to be repeated. It is this theory on which training methods are based today. For example, if you manipulate a dog to perform a specific behavior and reward him for doing it, he is likely to do it again because he enjoyed the end result.

Occasionally, punishment, a penalty inflicted for an offense, is necessary. The best type of punishment often comes from an outside source. For example, a child is told not to touch the stove because he may get burned. He disobeys and touches the stove. In doing so, he receives a burn. From that time on, he respects the heat of the stove and avoids contact with it. Therefore, a behavior that results in an unpleasant event tends not to be repeated.

THE CLEAN LIFE

By providing sleeping and resting quarters that fit the dog, and offering frequent opportunities to relieve himself outside his quarters, the puppy quickly learns that the outdoors is the place to go when he needs to urinate or defecate. It also reinforces his innate desire to keep his sleeping quarters clean. This, in turn, helps develop the muscle control that will eventually produce a dog with clean living habits.

With personalities as colorful as the rainbow of their coats, Greyhound pups are individuals and each may require a slightly different approach to training.

A good example of a dog's learning the hard way is the dog who chases the house cat. He is told many times to leave the cat alone, yet he persists in teasing the cat. Then, one day he begins chasing the cat but the cat turns and swipes a claw across the dog's face, leaving him with a painful gash on his nose. The final result is that the dog stops chasing the cat.

TRAINING EQUIPMENT

COLLAR AND LEAD
For a Greyhound, the collar and lead that you use for training must be one with which you are easily able to work, not too heavy for the dog and perfectly safe.

PRACTICE MAKES PERFECT!
- Have training lessons with your dog every day in several short segments—three to five times a day for a few minutes at a time is ideal.
- Do not have long practice sessions. The dog will become easily bored.
- Never practice when you are tired, ill, worried or in an otherwise negative mood. This will transmit to the dog and may have an adverse effect on his performance.

  Think fun, short and above all *positive!* End each session on a high note, rather than a failed exercise, and make sure to give a lot of praise. Enjoy the training and help your dog enjoy it, too.

Training leads and collars can be medium in strength and size, as Greyhounds are usually docile pets. Thin leads are usually best suited to the show ring and not for exercising the dog.

TREATS

Have a bag of treats on hand. Something nutritious and easy to swallow works best. Use a soft treat, a chunk of cheese or a piece of cooked chicken rather than a

---

PLAN TO PLAY

The puppy should also have regular play and exercise sessions when he is with you or a family member. Exercise for a very young puppy can consist of a short walk around the house or yard. Playing can include fetching games with a large ball or a special toy. (All puppies teethe and need soft things upon which to chew.) Remember to restrict play periods to indoors within his living area (the family room, for example) until he is completely house-trained.

---

dry biscuit. By the time the dog has finished chewing a dry treat, he will forget why he is being rewarded in the first place! Using food rewards will not teach a dog to beg at the table—the only way to teach a dog to beg at the table is to give him food from the table. In training, rewarding the dog with a food treat will help him associate praise and the treats with learning new behaviors that obviously please his owner.

TRAINING BEGINS: ASK THE DOG A QUESTION

In order to teach your dog anything, you must first get his attention. After all, he cannot learn anything if he is looking away from you with his mind on something else.

To get his attention, ask him "School?" and immediately walk over to him and give him a treat as you tell him "Good dog." Wait a minute or two and repeat the routine, this time with a treat in your hand as you approach within a foot of the dog. Do not go directly to him, but stop about a foot short of him and hold out the treat as you ask "School?" He will see you approaching with a treat in your hand and most likely begin walking toward you. As you meet, give him the treat and praise again.

The third time, ask the question, have a treat in your hand and walk only a short distance toward the dog so that he must walk almost all the way to you. As he reaches you, give him the treat and praise again.

By this time, the dog will probably be getting the idea that if he pays attention to you, especially when you ask that question, it will pay off in treats and enjoyable activities for him. In other words, he learns that "school" means doing great things with you that result in treats and positive attention for him.

Remember that the dog does not understand your verbal language, he only recognizes sounds. Your question translates to a series of sounds for him, and those sounds become the signal to go to you and pay attention; if he does, he will get to interact with you plus receive treats and praise.

THE BASIC COMMANDS

TEACHING SIT

Now that you have the dog's attention, attach his lead and hold it in your left hand and a food treat in your right. Place your food hand at the dog's nose and let him lick the treat but not take it from you. Say "Sit" and slowly raise your food hand from in front of the dog's nose up over his head so that he is looking at the ceiling. As he bends his head upward, he will have to bend his knees to maintain his balance. As he bends his knees, he will assume a sit

position. At that point, release the food treat and praise lavishly with comments such as "Good dog! Good sit!" Remember to always praise enthusiastically, because dogs relish verbal praise from their owners and feel so proud of themselves whenever they accomplish a behavior.

By the way, you will not use food forever in getting the dog to obey your commands. Food is only used to teach new behaviors, and once the dog knows what you want when you give a specific command, you will wean him off the food treats but still maintain the verbal praise. After all, you will always have your voice with you, and there will be many times when you have no food rewards but expect the dog to obey.

LANGUAGE BARRIER

Dogs do not understand our language and have to rely on tone of voice more than just words or sound. They can be trained to react to a certain sound, at a certain volume. If you say "No, Oliver" in a very soft, pleasant voice, it will not have the same meaning as "No, Oliver!!" when you raise your voice.

You should never use the dog's name during a reprimand, just the command "No! " You never want the dog to associate his name with a negative experience or reprimand.

TEACHING DOWN

Teaching the down exercise is easy when you understand how the dog perceives the down position, and it is very difficult when you do not. Dogs perceive the down position as a submissive one; therefore, teaching the down exercise using a forceful method can sometimes make the dog develop such a fear of the down that he either runs away when you say "Down" or he attempts to snap at the person who tries to force him down.

Have the dog sit close alongside your left leg, facing in the same direction as you are. Hold the lead in your left hand and a food treat in your right. Now place your left hand lightly on the top of the dog's shoulders where they meet above the spinal cord.

READY, SIT, GO!

On your marks, get set: train! Most professional trainers agree that the sit command is the place to start your dog's formal education. Sitting is a natural posture for most dogs and they respond to the sit exercise willingly and readily. For every lesson, begin with the sit command, so that you start out with a successful exercise. Likewise, you should practice the sit command at the end of every lesson as well because you always want to end on a high note.

Do not push down on the dog's shoulders; simply rest your left hand there so you can guide the dog to lie down close to your left leg rather than to swing away from your side when he drops.

Now place the food hand at the dog's nose, say "Down" very softly (almost a whisper) and slowly lower the food hand to the dog's front feet. When the food hand reaches the floor, begin moving it forward along the floor in front of the dog. Keep talking softly to the dog, saying things like, "Do you want this treat? You can do this, good dog." Your reassuring tone of voice will help calm the dog as he tries to follow the food hand in order to get the treat.

When the dog's elbows touch the floor, release the food and praise softly. Try to get the dog to maintain that down position for several seconds before you let him sit up again. The goal here is to get the dog to settle down and not feel threatened in the down position.

TEACHING STAY

It is easy to teach the dog to stay in either a sit or a down position. Again, we use food and praise during the teaching process as we help the dog to understand exactly what it is that we are expecting him to do.

To teach the sit/stay, start with the dog sitting on your left side as before and hold the lead in your left hand. Have a food treat in your right hand and place your food hand at the dog's nose. Say "Stay" and step out on your right foot to stand directly in front of the dog, toe to toe, as he licks and nibbles the treat. Be sure to keep his head facing upward to maintain the sit position. Count to five and then swing around to stand next to the dog again with him on your left. As soon as you get back to the original position, release the food and praise lavishly.

To teach the down/stay, do the down as previously described. As soon as the dog lies down, say "Stay" and step out on your right foot just as you did in the sit/stay. Count to five and then return to stand beside the dog with him on your left side. Release the treat and praise as always.

Within a week or ten days, you can begin to add a bit of distance between you and your dog when you leave him. When you do, use your left hand open with the palm facing the dog as a stay signal, much the same as the hand signal a police officer uses to stop traffic at an intersection. Hold the food treat in your right hand as before, but this time the food is not touching the dog's nose. He will watch the food hand and quickly learn that he is going to get that treat as soon as you return to his side.

When you can stand 3 feet away from your dog for 30 seconds, you can then begin building time and distance in both stays. Eventually, the dog can be expected to remain in the stay position for prolonged periods of time until you return to him or call him to you. Always praise lavishly when he stays.

TEACHING COME

If you make teaching "come" an exciting experience, you should never have a student that does not love the game or that fails to come when called. The secret, it seems, is never to teach the word "come."

At times when an owner most wants his dog to come when called, the owner is likely upset or anxious and he allows these feelings to come through in the tone of his voice when he calls his dog. Hearing that desperation in his owner's voice, the dog fears the results of going to him and

---

DOUBLE JEOPARDY

A dog in jeopardy never lies down. He stays alert on his feet because instinct tells him that he may have to run away or fight for his survival. Therefore, if a dog feels threatened or anxious, he will not lie down. Consequently, it is important to keep the dog calm and relaxed as he learns the down exercise.

Do not use your dog's name when teaching the stay command. Dogs likely want to move foward when they hear their names.

therefore either disobeys outright or runs in the opposite direction. The secret, therefore, is to teach the dog a game and, when you want him to come to you, simply play the game. It is practically a no-fail solution!

To begin, have several members of your family take a few food treats and each go into a different room in the house. Take turns calling the dog, and each

---

"WHERE ARE YOU?"

When calling the dog, do not say "Come." Say things like, "Rover, where are you? See if you can find me! I have a biscuit for you!" Keep up a constant line of chatter with coaxing sounds and frequent questions such as "Where are you?" The dog will learn to follow the sound of your voice to locate you and receive his reward.

---

person should celebrate the dog's finding him with a treat and lots of happy praise. When a person calls the dog, he is actually inviting the dog to find him and get a treat as a reward for "winning."

A few turns of the "Where are you?" game and the dog will figure out that everyone is playing the game and that each person has a big celebration awaiting his success at locating them. Once he learns to love the game, simply calling out "Where are you?" will bring the dog running from wherever he is when he hears that all-important question.

The come command is recognized as one of the most important things to teach a dog, but there are trainers who work with thousands of dogs and never teach the actual word "come." Yet these dogs will race to respond to a person who uses the dog's name followed by "Where are you?" For example, a woman has a 12-year-old companion dog who went blind, but who never fails to locate her owner when asked, "Where are you?"

Children particularly love to play this game with their dogs. Children can hide in smaller places like a shower stall or bathtub, behind a bed or under a table. The dog needs to work a little bit harder to find these hiding places, but, when he does, he loves to celebrate with a treat and a tussle with a favorite youngster.

"COME" ... BACK

Never call your dog to come to you for a correction or scold him when he reaches you. That is the quickest way to turn a come command into "Go away fast!" Dogs think only in the present tense, and your dog will connect the scolding with coming to you, not with the misbehavior of a few moments earlier.

TEACHING HEEL

Heeling means that the dog walks beside the owner without pulling. It takes time and patience on the owner's part to succeed at teaching the dog that he (the owner) will not proceed unless the dog is walking calmly beside him. Pulling out ahead on the lead is definitely not acceptable.

Begin with holding the lead in your left hand as the dog sits beside your left leg. Move the loop end of the lead to your right hand but keep your left hand

Your dog should become accustomed to being handled and standing politely if your ultimate goal is to enter dog shows. When teaching the dog to stand, you'll have to start by setting him in the correct position.

short on the lead so it keeps the dog in close next to you.

Say "Heel" and step forward on your left foot. Keep the dog close to you and take three steps. Stop and have the dog sit next to you in what we now call the heel position. Praise verbally, but do not touch the dog. Hesitate a moment and begin again with "Heel," taking three steps and stopping, at which point the dog is told to sit again.

Your goal here is to have the dog walk those three steps without pulling on the lead. Once he will walk calmly beside you for three steps without pulling, increase the number of steps you take to five. When he will walk politely beside you while you take five steps, you can increase the length of your walk to ten steps. Keep increasing the length of your stroll until the dog will walk quietly beside you without pulling as long as you want him to heel. When you stop heeling,

TUG OF WALK?
If you begin teaching the heel by taking long walks and letting the dog pull you along, he misinterprets this action as an acceptable form of taking a walk. When you pull back on the leash to counteract his pulling, he reads that tug as a signal to pull even harder!

indicate to the dog that the exercise is over by verbally praising as you pet him and say "OK, good dog." The "OK" is used as a release word, meaning that the exercise is finished and the dog is free to relax.

If you are dealing with a dog

convince the dog that you are the leader and you will be the one to decide on the direction and speed of your travel.

Each time the dog looks up at you or slows down to give a slack lead between the two of you, quietly praise him and say, "Good heel. Good dog." Eventually, the dog will begin to respond and within a few days he will be walking politely beside you without pulling on the lead. At first, the training sessions should be kept short and very positive; soon the dog will be able to walk nicely with you for increasingly longer distances. Remember also to give the dog free time and the opportunity to run and play when you are done with heel practice.

WEANING OFF FOOD IN TRAINING

Food is used in training new behaviors. Once the dog understands what behavior goes with a specific command, it is time to start weaning him off the food

Show dogs and pet dogs alike must master the heel command. Whether walking around the block or gaiting in the show ring, the Greyhound must respond invariably to the owner's command and gesture.

who insists on pulling you around, simply "put on your brakes" and stand your ground until the dog realizes that the two of you are not going anywhere until he is beside you and moving at your pace, not his. It may take some time just standing there to

HEELING WELL
Teach your dog to heel in an enclosed area. Once you think the dog will obey reliably and you want to attempt advanced obedience exercises such as off-lead heeling, test him in a fenced-in area so he cannot run away.

FEAR AGGRESSION

Pups who are subjected to physical abuse during training commonly end up with behavioral problems as adults. One common result of abuse is fear aggression, in which a dog will lash out, bare his teeth, snarl and finally bite someone by whom he feels threatened. For example, your daughter may be playing with the dog one afternoon. As they play hide-and-seek, she backs the dog into a corner and, as she attempts to tease him playfully, he bites her hand. Examine the cause of this behavior. Did your daughter ever hit the dog? Did someone who resembles your daughter hit or scream at the dog?

Fortunately, fear aggression is relatively easy to correct. Have your daughter engage in only positive activities with the dog, such as feeding, petting and walking. She should not give any corrections or negative feedback. If the dog still growls or cowers away from her, allow someone else to accompany them. After approximately one week, the dog should feel that he can rely on her for many positive things, and he will also be prevented from reacting fearfully towards anyone who might resemble her.

treats. At first, give a treat after each exercise. Then, start to give a treat only after every other exercise. Mix up the times when you offer a food reward and the times when you only offer praise so that the dog will never know when he is going to receive both food and praise and when he is going to receive only praise. This is called a variable-ratio reward system and it proves successful because there is always the chance that the owner will produce a treat, so the dog never stops trying for that reward. No matter what, *always* give verbal praise.

OBEDIENCE CLASSES

It is a good idea to enroll in an obedience class if one is available in your area. If yours is a show dog, conformation training classes would be more appropriate. Many

areas have dog clubs that offer basic obedience training as well as preparatory classes for obedience competition. There are also local dog trainers who offer similar classes.

At obedience trials, dogs can earn titles at various levels of competition. The beginning levels of competition include basic behaviors such as sit, down, heel, etc. The more advanced levels of competition include jumping, retrieving, scent discrimination and signal work. The advanced levels require a dog and owner to put a lot of time and effort into their training, and the titles that can be earned at these levels of competition are very prestigious.

OTHER ACTIVITIES FOR LIFE

Whether a dog is trained in the structured environment of a class or alone with his owner at home, there are many activities that can bring fun and rewards to both owner and dog once they have mastered basic control.

Teaching the dog to help out around the home, in the yard or on the farm provides great satisfaction to both dog and owner. In addition, the dog's help makes life a little easier for his owner and raises his stature as a valued companion to his family. It helps give the dog a purpose by occupying his mind and providing an outlet for his energy.

If you are interested in participating in organized competition with your Greyhound, there are activities other than obedience in which you and your dog can become involved. Greyhound owners have the opportunity of participating in sight-hound events with their dogs, including lure coursing and racing competitions. Lure-coursing events are sponsored by breed clubs, with

the sanction of the AKC. These exciting meets are designed to approximate a "live chase," though no rabbits are used. The lures are usually white in color (for sighting purposes) and covered in rabbit fur (for scenting purposes). Since the courses are drawn randomly, your dog must get along well with other dogs to participate. In addition to meeting other Greyhounds at these events, you may also meet Whippets, Rhodesian Ridgebacks, Salukis, Sloughis and other handsome sight hounds.

For racing events, contact the Large Gazehound Racing Association, the American Sighthound Field Association and other similar organizations that sponsor informal events for racing. These events can include even small sight hounds, like Italian Greyhounds! The AKC website features a search engine that can help you locate a local club that offers lure-coursing and racing events.

Agility is a popular sport where dogs run through an obstacle course that includes various jumps, tunnels and other exercises to test the dog's speed and coordination. The owners run through the course beside their dogs to give commands and to guide them through the course. Although competitive, the focus is on fun—it's fun to do, fun to watch and great exercise.

FAMILY TIES

If you have other pets in the home and/or interact often with the pets of friends and other family members, your pup will respond to those pets in much the same manner as you do. It is only when you show fear of or resentment toward another animal that he will act fearful or unfriendly.

Internal Organs of the Greyhound

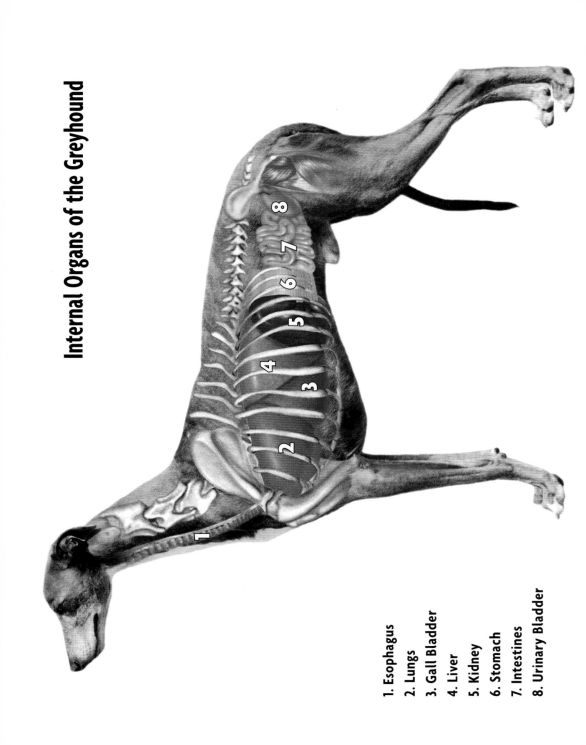

1. Esophagus
2. Lungs
3. Gall Bladder
4. Liver
5. Kidney
6. Stomach
7. Intestines
8. Urinary Bladder

Dogs can suffer from many of the same physical illnesses as people. They might even share many of the same psychological problems. Since people usually know more about human diseases than canine maladies, many of the terms used in this chapter will be familiar but not necessarily those used by veterinarians. We will use the term *x-ray*, instead of the more acceptable term *radiograph*. We will also use the familiar term *symptoms* even though dogs don't have symptoms, which are verbal descriptions of the patient's feelings; dogs have *clinical signs*. Since dogs can't speak, we have to look for clinical signs...but we still use the term *symptoms* in this book.

As a general rule, medicine is *practiced*. That term is not arbitrary. Medicine is a constantly changing art as we learn more and more about genetics, electronic aids (like

CAT scans and MRIs) and daily laboratory advances. There are many dog maladies, like canine hip dysplasia, which are not universally treated in the same manner. For example, some vets opt for surgery more often than others do.

SELECTING A VETERINARIAN
Your selection of a veterinarian should be based not only upon personality and ability with large breeds, Greyhounds or sight hounds but also upon his convenience to your home. You want a vet who is close because you might have emergencies or need to make multiple visits for treatments. You want a vet who has services that you might require such as tattooing and boarding facilities, who keeps up with the latest veterinary advances and who has a good reputation for ability

Your chosen vet should be familiar with the latest technologies and have all the necessary equipment at his disposal.

Breakdown of Veterinary Income by Category

2%	Dentistry
4%	Radiology
12%	Surgery
15%	Vaccinations
19%	Laboratory
23%	Examinations
25%	Medicines

A typical vet's income, categorized according to services performed. This survey dealt with small-animal (pets) practices.

and responsiveness. There is nothing more frustrating than having to wait a day or more to get a response from your vet.

All veterinarians are licensed and their diplomas and/or certificates should be displayed in their waiting rooms. Your vet will deal with your pet's routine health care and maintenance, injuries and illnesses, routine surgeries and the promotion of health (for example, by vaccination). There are, however, many veterinary specialties that require further studies and internships. Therse include specialists in heart problems (veterinary cardiologists), skin problems (veterinary dermatologists), tooth and gum problems (veterinary dentists), eye problems (veterinary ophthalmologists) and x-rays (veterinary radiologists), and vets who have specialties in bones, muscles or certain organs.

When the problem affecting

your dog is serious, it is not unusual or impudent to get another medical opinion, although it is courteous to advise the vets concerned about this. You might also want to compare costs among several veterinarians. Sophisticated health care and veterinary services can be very costly. It is not infrequent that important decisions are based upon financial considerations.

PREVENTATIVE MEDICINE

It is much easier, less costly and more effective to practice preventative medicine than to fight bouts of illness and disease. Properly bred puppies come from parents that were selected based upon their genetic-disease profiles. Their mother should have been vaccinated, free of all internal and external parasites and properly nourished. For these reasons, a visit to the veterinarian who cared for the dam is recommended. The dam can pass on disease resistance to her puppies, which can last for eight to ten weeks. She can also pass on parasites and many infections. That's why you should learn as much about the dam's health as you can.

WEANING TO BRINGING PUP HOME

Puppies should be weaned by the time they are about two months old. A puppy that remains for at least eight weeks with his dam and littermates usually adapts

Number-One Killer Disease in Dogs: CANCER

In every age, there is a word associated with a disease or plague that causes humans to shudder. In the 21st century, that word is "cancer." Just as cancer is the leading cause of death in humans, it claims nearly half the lives of dogs that die from a natural disease as well as half the dogs that die over the age of ten years.

Described as a genetic disease, cancer becomes a greater risk as the dog ages. Vets and dog owners have become increasingly aware of the threat of cancer to dogs. Statistics reveal that one dog in every five will develop cancer, the most common of which is skin cancer. Many cancers, including prostate, ovarian and breast cancer, can be avoided by spaying and neutering our dogs by the age of six months.

Early detection of cancer can save or extend a dog's life, so it is absolutely vital for owners to have their dogs examined by a qualified vet or oncologist immediately upon detection of any abnormality. Certain dietary guidelines have also proven to reduce the onset and spread of cancer. Foods based on fish rather than beef, due to the presence of Omega-3 fatty acids, are recommended. Other amino acids such as glutamine have significant benefits for canines, particularly those breeds that show a greater susceptibility to cancer.

Cancer management and treatments promise hope for future generations of canines. Since the disease is genetic, breeders should never breed a dog whose parents, grandparents and any related siblings have developed cancer. It is difficult to know whether to exclude an otherwise healthy dog from a breeding program, as the disease does not manifest itself until the dog's senior years.

RECOGNIZE CANCER WARNING SIGNS

Since early detection can possibly rescue your dog from becoming a cancer statistic, it is essential for owners to recognize the possible signs and seek the assistance of a qualified professional.

- Abnormal bumps or lumps that continue to grow
- Bleeding or discharge from any body cavity
- Persistent stiffness or lameness
- Recurrent sores or sores that do not heal
- Inappetence
- Breathing difficulties
- Weight loss
- Bad breath or odors
- General malaise and fatigue
- Eating and swallowing problems
- Difficulty urinating and defecating

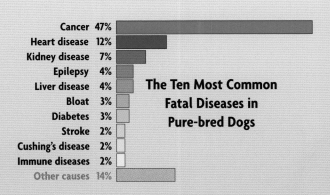

Cancer	47%
Heart disease	12%
Kidney disease	7%
Epilepsy	4%
Liver disease	4%
Bloat	3%
Diabetes	3%
Stroke	2%
Cushing's disease	2%
Immune diseases	2%
Other causes	14%

The Ten Most Common Fatal Diseases in Pure-bred Dogs

better to other dogs and people later in his life. Sometimes new owners have their puppies examined by the veterinarian immediately, which is a good idea; an appointment should be made for very soon after the pup's arrival home.

The puppy will have his teeth examined and have his skeletal conformation and general health checked prior to certification by the vet. Puppies in certain breeds have problems with their kneecaps, cataracts and other eye problems, heart murmurs and undescended testicles. Your vet might also have training in temperament evaluation. At the first visit, the vet will set up your pup's vaccination schedule.

VACCINATION SCHEDULING

Most vaccinations are given by injection and should only be done by a veterinarian. Both he and you should keep a record of the date of the injection, the identification of the vaccine and the amount given. Some vets give a first vaccination at six weeks, but most dog breeders prefer the course not to commence until about eight weeks because of negating any antibodies passed on by the dam. The vaccination scheduling is usually based on a 15-day cycle. You must take your veterinarian's advice as to when to vaccinate, as this may differ according to the vaccine used.

CUSHING'S DISEASE
Cases of hyperactive adrenal glands (Cushing's disease) have been traced to the drinking of highly chlorinated water. Aerate or age your dog's drinking water before offering it.

Most vaccinations immunize your puppy against viruses. The usual vaccines contain immunizing doses of several different viruses such as distemper, parvovirus, parainfluenza and hepatitis. There are other vaccines available when the puppy is at risk. You should rely upon professional advice. This is especially true for the booster-shot program. Most vaccination programs require a booster when the puppy is a year old and once a year thereafter. In some cases, circumstances may require more or less frequent immunizations. Canine cough, more formally known as tracheobronchitis, is treated with a vaccine that is sprayed into the dog's nostrils. Canine cough is usually included in routine vaccination, but this is often not as effective as the vaccines for other major diseases.

FIVE MONTHS TO ONE YEAR OF AGE

Unless you intend to breed or show your dog, neutering the puppy around six months of age is recommended. Discuss all aspects of the procedure with your veterinarian; most professionals advise neutering puppies that will not be shown or bred.

Neutering/spaying has proven to be extremely beneficial to male and female dogs, respectively. Besides eliminating the possibility of pregnancy and pyometra in bitches and testicular cancer in male dogs, it greatly reduces the

VACCINE ALLERGIES

Vaccines do not work all the time. Sometimes dogs are allergic to them and many times the antibodies, which are supposed to be stimulated by the vaccine, just are not produced. You should keep your dog in the veterinary clinic for an hour after he is vaccinated to be sure there are no allergic reactions.

HEALTH AND VACCINATION SCHEDULE

AGE IN WEEKS:	6TH	8TH	10TH	12TH	14TH	16TH	20-24TH	52ND
Worm Control	✔	✔	✔	✔	✔	✔	✔	
Neutering							✔	
Heartworm		✔		✔		✔	✔	
Parvovirus	✔		✔		✔		✔	✔
Distemper		✔		✔		✔		✔
Hepatitis		✔		✔		✔		✔
Leptospirosis								✔
Parainfluenza	✔		✔		✔			✔
Dental Examination		✔					✔	✔
Complete Physical		✔					✔	✔
Coronavirus				✔			✔	✔
Canine Cough	✔							
Hip Dysplasia								✔
Rabies							✔	

Vaccinations are not instantly effective. It takes about two weeks for the dog's immune system to develop antibodies. Most vaccinations require annual booster shots. Your vet should guide you in this regard.

PHARMACEUTICAL FIX

There are two drugs specifically designed to treat mental problems in dogs. About seven million dogs each year are destroyed because owners can no longer tolerate their dogs' behavior, according to Nicholas Dodman, a specialist in animal behavior at Tufts University in Massachusetts.

The first drug, Clomicalm, is prescribed for dogs suffering from separation anxiety, which is said to cause them to react when left alone by barking, chewing their owners' belongings, drooling copiously or defecating or urinating inside the home.

The second drug, Anipryl, is recommended for cognitive dysfunction syndrome or "old-dog syndrome," a mental deterioration that comes with age. Such dogs often seem to forget that they were housebroken and where their food bowls are, and they may even fail to recognize their owners.

A tremendous human-animal bonding relationship is established with all dogs, particularly senior dogs. This precious relationship deteriorates when the dog does not recognize his master. The drug can restore the bond and make senior dogs feel more like their "old selves."

risk of breast cancer in bitches and prostate cancer in male dogs.

DOGS OLDER THAN ONE YEAR
Continue to visit the veterinarian at least once a year. There is no such disease as old age, but bodily functions do change with age. The eyes and ears are no longer as efficient. Liver, kidney and intestinal functions often decline. Proper dietary changes, recommended by your veterinarian, can make life more pleasant for the aging Greyhound and you.

SKIN PROBLEMS IN GREYHOUNDS
Veterinarians are consulted by dog owners for skin problems more than for any other group of

diseases or maladies. Dogs' skin is almost as sensitive as human skin and both can suffer from almost the same ailments (though the occurrence of acne in most dogs is rare). For this reason, veterinary dermatology has developed into a specialty practiced by many veterinarians.

Since many skin problems have visual symptoms that are almost identical, it requires the skill of an experienced veterinary dermatologist to identify and cure many of the more severe skin disorders. Pet shops sell many treatments for skin problems, but most of the treatments are directed at symptoms and not the underlying problem(s). If your dog is suffering from a skin disorder, you should seek professional assistance as quickly as possible. As with all diseases, the earlier a problem is identified and treated, the more likely it is that the cure will be successful.

HEREDITARY SKIN DISORDERS

Veterinary dermatologists are currently researching a number of skin disorders that are believed to have hereditary bases. These inherited diseases are transmitted by both parents, who appear (phenotypically) normal but have

The "great outdoors" can be great fun for your Greyhound, but can also be a source of allergies, parasites and other irritants. Check your Greyhound's skin and coat regularly for any evidence of a problem.

DISEASE REFERENCE CHART

	What is it?	What causes it?	Symptoms
Leptospirosis	Severe disease that affects the internal organs; can be spread to people.	A bacterium, which is often carried by rodents, that enters through mucous membranes and spreads quickly throughout the body.	Range from fever, vomiting and loss of appetite in less severe cases to shock, irreversible kidney damage and possibly death in most severe cases.
Rabies	Potentially deadly virus that infects warm-blooded mammals.	Bite from a carrier of the virus, mainly wild animals.	1st stage: dog exhibits change in behavior, fear. 2nd stage: dog's behavior becomes more aggressive. 3rd stage: loss of coordination, trouble with bodily functions.
Parvovirus	Highly contagious virus, potentially deadly.	Ingestion of the virus, which is usually spread through the feces of infected dogs.	Most common: severe diarrhea. Also vomiting, fatigue, lack of appetite.
Canine cough	Contagious respiratory infection.	Combination of types of bacteria and virus. Most common: *Bordetella bronchiseptica* bacteria and parainfluenza virus.	Chronic cough.
Distemper	Disease primarily affecting respiratory and nervous system.	Virus that is related to the human measles virus.	Mild symptoms such as fever, lack of appetite and mucus secretion progress to evidence of brain damage, "hard pad."
Hepatitis	Virus primarily affecting the liver.	Canine adenovirus type I (CAV-1). Enters system when dog breathes in particles.	Lesser symptoms include listlessness, diarrhea, vomiting. More severe symptoms include "blue-eye" (clumps of virus in eye).
Coronavirus	Virus resulting in digestive problems.	Virus is spread through infected dog's feces.	Stomach upset evidenced by lack of appetite, vomiting, diarrhea.

a recessive gene for the disease, meaning that they carry, but are not affected by, the disease. These diseases pose serious problems to breeders because in some instances there are no methods of identifying carriers, although the occurrence of these diseases in Greyhounds is not too common. Sometimes the secondary diseases associated with these skin conditions are even more debilitating than the skin disorders themselves, including cancers and respiratory problems.

Among the hereditary skin disorders, for which the mode of inheritance is known, are acrodermatitis, cutaneous asthenia (Ehlers-Danlos syndrome), sebaceous adenitis, cyclic hematopoiesis, dermatomyositis, IgA deficiency, color dilution alopecia and nodular dermatofibrosis. Some of these disorders are limited to one or two breeds, while others affect a large number of breeds. If you detect any growths or other abnormalities on your Greyhound's skin or coat, report this to your veterinarian immediately. All inherited diseases must be diagnosed and treated by a veterinary specialist.

PARASITE BITES

Many of us are allergic to insect bites. The bites itch, erupt and may even become infected. Dogs have the same reaction to fleas, ticks and/or mites. When an

---

"P" STANDS FOR PROBLEM

Urinary-tract disease is a serious condition that requires immediate medical attention. Symptoms include urinating in inappropriate places or the need to urinate frequently in small amounts. Urinary-tract disease is most effectively treated with antibiotics. To help promote good urinary-tract health, owners must always be sure that a constant supply of fresh water is available to their pets.

---

insect lands on you, you have the chance to whisk it away with your hand. Unfortunately, when your dog is bitten by a flea, tick or mite, he can only scratch it away or bite it. By the time the dog has been bitten, the parasite has done some of its damage. It may also have laid eggs to cause further problems in the near future. The itching from parasite bites is probably due to the saliva injected into the site when the parasite sucks the dog's blood.

AUTO-IMMUNE SKIN CONDITIONS

Auto-immune skin conditions are commonly referred to as being allergic to yourself, while allergies are usually inflammatory reactions to an outside stimulus. Auto-immune diseases cause serious damage to the tissues that are involved.

The best known auto-immune

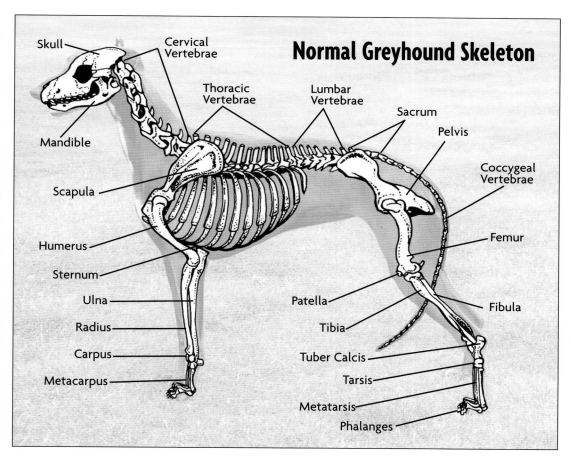

Normal Greyhound Skeleton

Skull
Cervical Vertebrae
Thoracic Vertebrae
Lumbar Vertebrae
Sacrum
Pelvis
Mandible
Coccygeal Vertebrae
Scapula
Humerus
Sternum
Femur
Ulna
Radius
Carpus
Patella
Tibia
Fibula
Metacarpus
Tuber Calcis
Tarsis
Metatarsis
Phalanges

disease is lupus, which affects people as well as dogs. The symptoms are variable and may affect the kidneys, bones, blood chemistry and skin. It can be fatal to both dogs and humans, though it is not thought to be transmissible. It is usually successfully treated with cortisone, prednisone or similar corticosteroid, but extensive use of these drugs can have harmful side effects.

MANY KINDS OF EARS
Not every dog's ears are the same. Ears that are open to the air are healthier than ears with poor air circulation. Sometimes a dog can have two differently shaped ears. You should not probe inside your dog's ears. Only clean that which is accessible with a cotton ball.

DENTAL HEALTH

A dental examination is in order when the dog is between six months and one year of age so that any permanent teeth that have erupted incorrectly can be corrected. It is important to begin a brushing routine at home, using dental-care products made for dogs, such as special toothbrushes and toothpaste. Durable nylon and safe edible chews should be a part of your puppy's arsenal for good health, good teeth and pleasant breath. The vast majority of dogs three to four years old and older has diseases of the gums from lack of dental attention. Using the various types of dental chews can be very effective in controlling dental plaque.

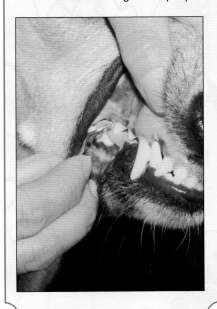

ACRAL LICK GRANULOMA

Many large dogs have a very poorly understood syndrome called acral lick granuloma. The manifestation of the problem is the dog's tireless attack at a specific area of the body, almost always the legs or paws. The dog licks so intensively that he removes the hair and skin, leaving an ugly, large wound. Tiny protuberances, which are outgrowths of new capillaries, bead on the surface of the wound. Owners who notice their dogs' biting and chewing at their extremities should have the vet determine the cause. If lick granuloma is the cause, although there is no absolute cure, corticosteroids are the most common treatment.

AIRBORNE ALLERGIES

Just as humans have hay fever, rose fever and other fevers from which they suffer during the pollinating season, many dogs suffer from the same allergies. When the pollen count is high, your dog might suffer, but don't expect him to sneeze and have a runny nose as you would. Dogs react to pollen allergies the same way they react to fleas—they scratch and bite themselves.

Dogs, like humans, can be tested for allergens. Discuss the testing with your veterinary dermatologist.

FOOD PROBLEMS

FOOD ALLERGIES

Dogs can be allergic to many foods that are best-sellers and highly recommended by breeders and veterinarians. Changing the brand of food that you buy may not eliminate the problem if the element to which the dog is allergic is contained in the new brand.

Recognizing a food allergy is difficult. Humans vomit or have rashes when they eat a food to

This telltale wound is the result of acral lick granuloma, caused by the dog's constant licking at the same spot on his leg.

SIMULATED MEDICAL CONDITION FOR EDUCATIONAL PURPOSES ONLY.

which they are allergic. Dogs neither vomit nor (usually) develop a rash. They react in the same manner as they do to an airborne or flea allergy: they itch, scratch and bite, thus making the diagnosis extremely difficult. While pollen allergies and parasite bites are usually seasonal, food allergies are year-round problems.

FOOD INTOLERANCE

Food intolerance is the inability of the dog to completely digest certain foods. A common scenario involves puppies that may have done very well on their mother's milk, but may not do well on cow's milk. The result of this food intolerance may be loose bowels, passing gas and stomach pains. These are the only obvious symptoms

PET ADVANTAGES

If you do not intend to show or breed your new puppy, your veterinarian will probably recommend that you spay your female or neuter your male. Some people believe neutering leads to weight gain, but if you feed and exercise your dog properly, this is easily avoided. Spaying or neutering can actually have many positive outcomes, such as:

• training becomes easier, as the dog focuses less on the urge to mate and more on you!

• females are protected from unplanned pregnancy as well as ovarian and uterine cancers.

• males are guarded from testicular tumors and have a reduced risk of developing prostate cancer.

Talk to your vet regarding the right age to spay/neuter and other aspects of the procedure.

Pups get a good nutritional start in life from nursing from their mother. Once weaned, a good-quality balanced puppy food should provide them with the nutrition they need.

of food intolerance, and that makes diagnosis difficult.

TREATING FOOD PROBLEMS

It is possible to handle food allergies and food intolerance yourself. Put your dog on a diet that he has never had. Obviously if he has never eaten this new food, he can't yet have been allergic or intolerant of it. Start with a single ingredient that is not in the dog's diet at the present time. Ingredients like chopped beef or chicken are common in dog's diets, so try something different like lamb,

DON'T EAT THE DAISIES!

Many plants and flowers are beautiful to look at, but can be highly toxic if ingested by your dog. Reactions range from abdominal pain and vomiting to convulsions and death. If the following plants are in your home, remove them. If they are outside your house or in your garden, avoid accidents by making sure your dog is never left unsupervised in those locations.

Azalea	Dumb cane	Mescal bean
Belladonna	Dutchman's breeches	Mushrooms
Bird of paradise	Elephant's ear	Nightshade
Bulbs	Hydrangea	Philodendron
Calla lily	Jack-in-the-pulpit	Poinsettia
Cardinal flower	Jasmine	*Prunus* species
Castor bean	Jimsonweed	Tobacco
Chinaberry tree	Larkspur	Yellow jasmine
Daphne	Laurel	Yews, *Taxus* species
	Lily of the valley	

VITAMIN POSSIBILITIES FOR DOGS

Some breeders and vets recommend the supplementation of vitamins to a dog's diet—others do not. Before embarking on a vitamin program, consult your vet.

Vitamin / Dosage	Food source	Benefits
A / 10,000 IU/week	Eggs, butter, yogurt, meat	Skin, eyes, hind legs, haircoat
B / Varies	Organs, cottage cheese, sardines	Appetite, fleas, heart, skin and coat
C / 2000 mg+	Fruit, legumes, leafy green vegetables	Healing, arthritis, kidneys
D / Varies	Cod liver oil, cheese, organs, eggs	Bones, teeth, endocrine system
E / 250 IU daily	Leafy green vegetables, meat, wheat germ oil	Skin, muscles, nerves, healing, digestion
F / Varies	Fish oils, raw meat	Heart, skin, coat, fleas
K / Varies	Naturally in body, not through food	Blood clotting

fish or another protein source. Keep the dog on this diet (with no additives) for a month. If the symptoms of food allergy or intolerance disappear, chances are your dog has a food allergy.

Don't think that the single ingredient cured the problem. You still must find a suitable diet and ascertain which ingredient in the old diet was objectionable. This is most easily done by adding ingredients to the new diet one at a time. Let the dog stay on the modified diet for a month before you add another ingredient. Eventually, you will determine the ingredient that caused the adverse reaction.

An alternative method is to study the ingredients in the diet to which your dog is allergic or intolerant. Identify the main ingredient in this diet and eliminate the main ingredient by buying a different food that does not have that ingredient. Keep experimenting until the symptoms disappear after one month on the new diet.

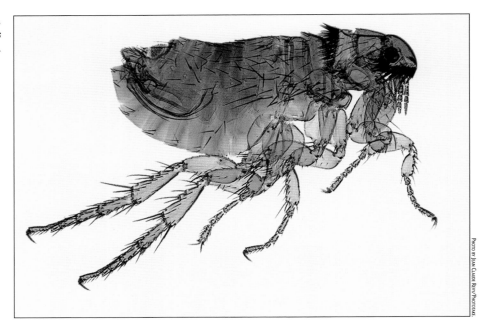

A male dog flea, *Ctenocephalides canis.*

PHOTO BY JEAN CLAUDE REVY/PHOTOTAKE.

EXTERNAL PARASITES

FLEAS

Of all the problems to which dogs are prone, none is more well known and frustrating than fleas. Flea infestation is relatively simple to cure but difficult to prevent. Parasites that are harbored inside the body are a bit more difficult to eradicate but they are easier to control.

To control flea infestation, you have to understand the flea's life cycle. Fleas are often thought of as a summertime problem, but centrally heated homes have changed the patterns and fleas can be found at any time of the year. The most effective method of flea control is a two-stage approach: one stage to kill the adult fleas, and the other to control the development of pre-adult fleas. Unfortunately, no single active ingredient is effective against all stages of the life cycle.

FLEA KILLER CAUTION— "POISON"

Flea-killers are poisonous. You should not spray these toxic chemicals on areas of a dog's body that he licks, including his genitals and his face. Flea killers taken internally are a better answer, but check with your vet in case internal therapy is not advised for your dog.

LIFE CYCLE STAGES

During its life, a flea will pass through four life stages: egg, larva, pupa or nymph and adult. The adult stage is the most visible and irritating stage of the flea life cycle, and this is why the majority of flea-control products concentrate on this stage. The fact is that adult fleas account for only 1% of the total flea population, and the other 99% exist in pre-adult stages, i.e., eggs, larvae and nymphs. The pre-adult stages are barely visible to the naked eye.

THE LIFE CYCLE OF THE FLEA

Eggs are laid on the dog, usually in quantities of about 20 or 30, several times a day. The adult female flea must have a blood meal before each egg-laying session. When first laid, the eggs will cling to the dog's hair, as the eggs are still moist. However, they will quickly dry out and fall from the dog, especially if the dog moves around or scratches. Many eggs will fall off in the dog's favorite area or an area in which he spends a lot of time, such as his bed.

Once the eggs fall from the dog onto the carpet or furniture, they will hatch into larvae. This takes from one to ten days. Larvae are not particularly mobile and will usually travel only a few inches from where they hatch. However, they do have a tendency to move away from bright light and heavy

EN GARDE:
CATCHING FLEAS OFF GUARD!

Consider the following ways to arm yourself against fleas:

- Add a small amount of pennyroyal or eucalyptus oil to your dog's bath. These natural remedies repel fleas.
- Supplement your dog's food with fresh garlic (minced or grated) and a hearty amount of brewer's yeast, both of which ward off fleas.
- Use a flea comb on your dog daily. Submerge fleas in a cup of bleach to kill them quickly.
- Confine the dog to only a few rooms to limit the spread of fleas in the home.
- Vacuum daily...and get all of the crevices! Dispose of the bag every few days until the problem is under control.
- Wash your dog's bedding daily. Cover cushions where your dog sleeps with towels, and wash the towels often.

traffic—under furniture and behind doors are common places to find high quantities of flea larvae.

The flea larvae feed on dead organic matter, including adult flea feces, until they are ready to change into adult fleas. Fleas will usually remain as larvae for around seven days. After this period, the larvae will pupate into protective pupae. While inside the pupae, the larvae will undergo

Fleas have been measured as being able to jump 300,000 times and can jump over 150 times their length in any direction, including straight up.

metamorphosis and change into adult fleas. This can take as little time as a few days, but the adult fleas can remain inside the pupae waiting to hatch for up to two years. The pupae are signaled to hatch by certain stimuli, such as physical pressure—the pupae's being stepped on, heat from an animal's lying on the pupae or increased carbon-dioxide levels and vibrations—indicating that a suitable host is available.

Once hatched, the adult flea must feed within a few days. Once the adult flea finds a host, it will not leave voluntarily. It only becomes dislodged by grooming or the host animal's scratching.

A scanning electron micrograph of a dog or cat flea, *Ctenocephalides*, magnified more than 100x. This image has been colorized for effect.

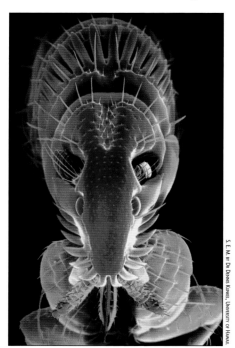

The adult flea will remain on the host for the duration of its life unless forcibly removed.

TREATING THE ENVIRONMENT AND THE DOG

Treating fleas should be a two-pronged attack. First, the environment needs to be treated; this includes carpets and furniture, especially the dog's bedding and areas underneath furniture. The environment should be treated with a household spray containing an Insect Growth Regulator (IGR) and an insecticide to kill the adult fleas. Most IGRs are effective against eggs and larvae; they actually mimic the fleas' own hormones and stop the eggs and larvae from developing into adult fleas. There are currently no treatments available to attack the pupa stage of the life cycle, so the adult insecticide is used to kill the newly hatched adult fleas before they find a host. Most IGRs are active for many months, while

THE LIFE CYCLE OF THE FLEA

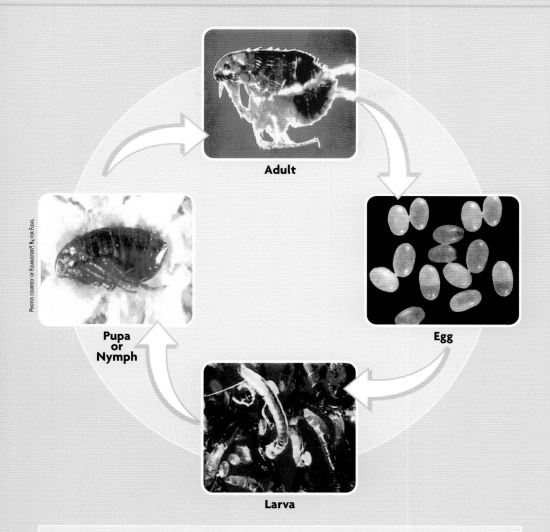

Adult

Egg

Larva

Pupa or Nymph

Fleas have been around for millions of years and have adapted to changing host animals. They are able to go through a complete life cycle in less than one month or they can extend their lives to almost two years by remaining as pupae or cocoons. They do not need blood or any other food for up to 20 months.

INSECT GROWTH REGULATOR (IGR)

Two types of products should be used when treating fleas—a product to treat the pet and a product to treat the home. Adult fleas represent less than 1% of the flea population. The pre-adult fleas (eggs, larvae and pupae) represent more than 99% of the flea population and are found in the environment; it is in the case of pre-adult fleas that products containing an Insect Growth Regulator (IGR) should be used in the home.

IGRs are a new class of compounds used to prevent the development of insects. They do not kill the insect outright, but instead use the insect's biology against it to stop it from completing its growth. Products that contain methoprene are the world's first and leading IGRs. Used to control fleas and other insects, this type of IGR will stop flea larvae from developing and protect the house for up to seven months.

The American dog tick, *Dermacentor variabilis,* **is probably the most common tick found on dogs. Look at the strength in its eight legs! No wonder it's hard to detach them.**

The second stage of treatment is to apply an adult insecticide to the dog. Traditionally, this would be in the form of a collar, which prove harmful to the Greyhound. Likewise, digestible insecticides that poison the fleas when they ingest the dog's blood are also not advised for the Greyhound. Avoid any treatment that uses organo-phosphates. Alternatively, there are drops that, when placed on the back of the dog's neck, spread throughout the hair and skin to kill adult fleas.

TICKS

Though not as common as fleas, ticks are found all over the tropical and temperate world. They don't bite, like fleas; they harpoon. They dig their sharp

adult insecticides are only active for a few days.

When treating with a house-hold spray, it is a good idea to vacuum before applying the product. This stimulates as many pupae as possible to hatch into adult fleas. The vacuum cleaner should also be treated with an insecticide to prevent the eggs and larvae that have been collected in the vacuum bag from hatching.

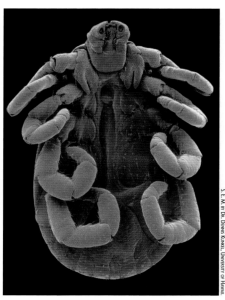

S. E. M. BY DR. DENNIS KUNKEL, UNIVERSITY OF HAWAII

proboscis (nose) into the dog's skin and drink the blood. Their only food and drink is dog's blood. Dogs can get Lyme disease, Rocky Mountain spotted fever, tick bite paralysis and many other diseases from ticks. They may live where fleas are found and they like to hide in cracks or seams in walls. They are controlled the same way fleas are controlled.

The American dog tick, *Dermacentor variabilis*, may well be the most common dog tick in many geographical areas, especially those areas where the climate is hot and humid. Most dog ticks have life expectancies of a week to six months, depending upon climatic conditions. They can neither jump nor fly, but they can crawl slowly and can range up to 16 feet to reach a sleeping or unsuspecting dog.

MITES

Just as fleas and ticks can be problematic for your dog, mites can also lead to an itchy nuisance. Microscopic in size, mites are related to ticks and generally take up permanent residence on their host animal—in this case, your dog! The term *mange* refers to any infestation caused by one of the mighty mites, of which there are six varieties that concern dog owners.

Demodex mites cause a condition known as demodicosis

DEER-TICK CROSSING

The great outdoors may be fun for your dog, but it also is a home to dangerous ticks. Deer ticks carry a bacterium known as *Borrelia burgdorferi* and are most active in the autumn and spring. When infections are caught early, penicillin and tetracycline are effective antibiotics, but, if left untreated, the bacteria may cause neurological, kidney and cardiac problems as well as long-term trouble with walking and painful joints.

S. E. M. BY DR. ANDREW SPIELMAN/PHOTOTAKE.

PHOTO BY DR. DENNIS KUNKEL, UNIVERSITY OF HAWAII.

The head of an American dog tick, *Dermacentor variabilis*, enlarged and colorized for effect.

The mange mite, *Psoroptes bovis*, can infest cattle and other domestic animals.

PHOTO BY JAMES HAYDEN/YOAV/PHOTOTAKE.

(sometimes called red mange or follicular mange), in which the mites live in the dog's hair follicles and sebaceous glands in larger-than-normal numbers. This type of mange is commonly passed from the dam to her puppies and usually shows up on the puppies' muzzles, though demodicosis is not transferable from one normal dog to another. Most dogs recover from this type of mange without any treatment, though topical therapies are commonly prescribed by the vet.

Human lice look like dog lice; the two are closely related.
PHOTO BY DWIGHT R. KUHN.

The *Cheyletiellosis* mite is the hook-mouthed culprit associated with "walking dandruff," a condition that affects dogs as well as cats and rabbits. This mite lives on the surface of the animal's skin and is readily transferable through direct or indirect contact with an affected animal. The dandruff is present in the form of scaly skin, which may or may not be itchy. If not treated, this mange can affect a whole kennel of dogs and can be spread to humans as well.

The *Sarcoptes* mite causes intense itching on the dog in the form of a condition known as scabies or sarcoptic mange. The cycle of the *Sarcoptes* mite lasts about three weeks, and the mites live in the top layer of the dog's skin (epidermis), preferably in areas with little hair. Scabies is highly contagious and can be passed to humans. Sometimes an allergic reaction to the mite worsens the severe itching associated with sarcoptic mange.

Ear mites, *Otodectes cynotis,* lead to otodectic mange, which most commonly affects the outer ear canal of the dog, though other areas can be affected as well. Dogs with ear-mite infestation commonly scratch at their ears, causing further irritation, and shake their heads. Dark brown droppings in the outer ear confirm the diagnosis. Your vet can prescribe a treatment to flush out the ears and kill any eggs in the ears. A complete month of treatment is necessary to cure the mange.

Two other mites, less common in dogs, include *Dermanyssus gallinae* (the poultry or red mite) and *Eutrombicula alfreddugesi* (the North American mite associated with trombiculidiasis or chigger infestation). The poultry mite frequently lives on chickens, but can transfer to dogs who spend

DO NOT MIX
Never mix parasite-control products without first consulting your vet. Some products can become toxic when combined with others and can cause fatal consequences.

NOT A DROP TO DRINK
Never allow your dog to swim in polluted water or public areas where water quality can be suspect. Even perfectly clear water can harbor parasites, many of which can cause serious to fatal illnesses in canines. Areas inhabited by waterfowl and other wildlife are especially dangerous.

time near farm animals. Chigger infestation affects dogs in the central US who have exposure to woodlands. The types of mange caused by both of these mites are treatable by vets.

INTERNAL PARASITES
Most animals—fishes, birds and mammals, including dogs and humans—have worms and other parasites that live inside their bodies. According to Dr. Herbert R. Axelrod, the fish pathologist, there are two kinds of parasites: dumb and smart. The smart parasites live in peaceful cooperation with their hosts (symbiosis), while the dumb parasites kill their hosts. Most worm infections are relatively easy to control. If they are not controlled, they weaken the host dog to the point that other medical problems occur, but they do not kill the host as dumb parasites would.

A brown dog tick, *Rhipicephalus sanguineus,* **is an uncommon but annoying tick found on dogs.**

Photo by Carolina Biological Supply/Phototake

The roundworm *Rhabditis* can infect both dogs and humans.

The roundworm, *Ascaris lumbricoides.*

ROUNDWORMS

Average-size dogs can pass 1,360,000 roundworm eggs every day. For example, if there were only 1 million dogs in the world, the world would be saturated with thousands of tons of dog feces. These feces would contain around 15,000,000,000 roundworm eggs.

Up to 31% of home yards and children's sand boxes in the US contain roundworm eggs.

Flushing dog's feces down the toilet is not a safe practice because the usual sewage treatments do not destroy roundworm eggs.

Infected puppies start shedding roundworm eggs at three weeks of age. They can be infected by their mother's milk.

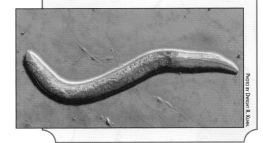

Photo by Dwight R. Kuhn

ROUNDWORMS

The roundworms that infect dogs are known scientifically as *Toxocara canis.* They live in the dog's intestines and shed eggs continually. It has been estimated that a dog produces about 6 or more ounces of feces every day. Each ounce of feces averages hundreds of thousands of roundworm eggs. There are no known areas in which dogs roam that do not contain roundworm eggs. The greatest danger of roundworms is that they infect people, too! It is wise to have your dog tested regularly for roundworms.

In young puppies, roundworms cause bloated bellies, diarrhea, coughing and vomiting, and are transmitted from the dam (through blood or milk). Affected puppies will not appear as animated as normal puppies. The worms appear spaghetti-like, measuring as long as 6 inches. Adult dogs can acquire roundworms through coprophagia (eating contaminated feces) or by killing rodents that carry roundworms.

Roundworm infection can kill puppies and cause severe problems in adults, as the hatched larvae travel to the lungs and trachea through the bloodstream. Cleanliness is the best preventative for roundworms. Always pick up after your dog and dispose of feces in appropriate receptacles.

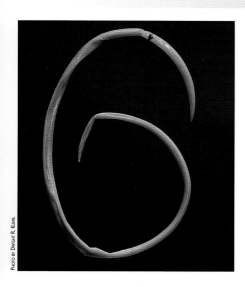

HOOKWORMS

In the United States, dog owners have to be concerned about four different species of hookworm, the most common and most serious of which is *Ancylostoma caninum*, which prefers warm climates. The others are *Ancylostoma braziliense*, *Ancylostoma tubaeforme* and *Uncinaria stenocephala*, the latter of which is a concern to dogs living in the northern US and Canada, as this species prefers cold climates.

Hookworms are dangerous to humans as well as to dogs and cats, and can be the cause of severe anemia due to iron deficiency. The worm uses its teeth to attach itself to the dog's intestines and changes the site of its attachment about six times per day. Each time the worm repositions itself, the dog loses blood and can become anemic. *Ancylostoma caninum* is the most likely of the four species to cause anemia in the dog.

Symptoms of hookworm infection include dark stools, weight loss, general weakness, pale coloration and anemia, as well as possible skin problems. Fortunately, hookworms are easily purged from the affected dog with a number of medications that have proven effective. Discuss these with your vet. Most heartworm preventatives include a hookworm insecticide as well.

Owners also must be aware that hookworms can infect humans, who can acquire the larvae through exposure to contaminated feces. Since the worms cannot complete their life cycle on a human, the worms simply infest the skin and cause irritation. This condition is known as cutaneous larva migrans syndrome. As a preventative, use disposable gloves or a "poop-scoop" to pick up your dog's droppings and prevent your dog (or neighborhood cats) from defecating in children's play areas.

The hookworm, *Ancylostoma caninum*.

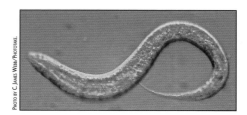

The infective stage of the hookworm larva.

TAPEWORMS

Humans, rats, squirrels, foxes, coyotes, wolves and domestic dogs are all susceptible to tapeworm infection. Except in humans, tapeworms are usually not a fatal infection. Infected individuals can harbor 1000 parasitic worms.

Tapeworms, like some other types of worm, are hermaphroditic, meaning male and female in the same worm.

If dogs eat infected rats or mice, or anything else infected with tapeworm, they get the tapeworm disease. One month after attaching to a dog's intestine, the worm starts shedding eggs. These eggs are infective immediately. Infective eggs can live for a few months without a host animal.

The head and rostellum (the round prominence on the scolex) of a tapeworm, which infects dogs and humans.

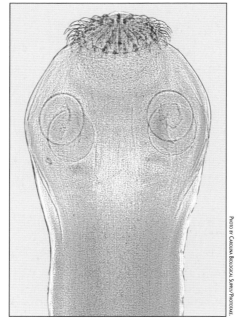

PHOTO BY CAROLINA BIOLOGICAL SUPPLY/PHOTOTAKE.

TAPEWORMS

There are many species of tapeworm, all of which are carried by fleas! The most common tapeworm affecting dogs is known as *Dipylidium caninum*. The dog eats the flea and starts the tapeworm cycle. Humans can also be infected with tapeworms—so don't eat fleas! Fleas are so small that your dog could pass them onto your hands, your plate or your food and thus make it possible for you to ingest a flea that is carrying tapeworm eggs.

While tapeworm infection is not life-threatening in dogs (smart parasite!), it can be the cause of a very serious liver disease for humans. About 50% of the humans infected with *Echinococcus multilocularis*, a type of tapeworm that causes alveolar hydatid, perish.

WHIPWORMS

In North America, whipworms are counted among the most common parasitic worms in dogs. The whipworm's scientific name is *Trichuris vulpis*. These worms attach themselves in the lower parts of the intestine, where they feed. Affected dogs may only experience upset tummies, colic and diarrhea. These worms, however, can live for months or years in the dog, beginning their larval stage in the small intestine, spending their adult stage in the large intestine and finally passing infective eggs through the dog's feces. The only way to detect whipworms is through a fecal examination, though this is not always foolproof. Treatment for whipworms is tricky, due to the worms' unusual life-cycle pattern, and very often dogs are reinfected due to exposure to infective eggs on the ground. The whipworm eggs can survive in the environment for as long as five years; thus, cleaning up droppings in your own backyard as well as in public places is absolutely essential for sanitation purposes and the health of your dog and others.

THREADWORMS

Though less common than round-worms, hookworms and those previously mentioned, thread-worms concern dog owners in the southwestern US and Gulf Coast area where the climate is hot and humid. Living in the small intestine of the dog, this worm measures a mere 2 millimeters and is round in shape. Like that of the whipworm, the threadworm's life cycle is very complex and the eggs and larvae are passed through the feces. A deadly disease in humans, *Strongyloides* readily infects people, and the handling of feces is the most common means of transmission. Threadworms are most often seen in young puppies; bloody diarrhea and pneumonia are symptoms. Sick puppies must be isolated and treated immediately; vets recommend a follow-up treatment one month later.

HEARTWORM PREVENTATIVES

There are many heartworm preventatives on the market, many of which are sold at your veterinarian's office. These products can be given daily or monthly, depending on the manufacturer's instructions. All of these preventatives contain chemical insecticides directed at killing heartworms, which leads to some controversy among dog owners. In effect, heartworm preventatives are necessary evils, though you should determine how necessary based on your pet's lifestyle. There is no doubt that heartworm is a dreadful disease that threatens the lives of dogs. However, the likelihood of your dog's being bitten by an infected mosquito is slim in most places, and a mosquito-repellent (or an herbal remedy such as Wormwood or Black Walnut) is much safer for your dog and will not compromise his immune system (the way heartworm preventatives will). Should you decide to use the traditional preventative "medications," you can consider giving the pill every other or third month. Since the toxins in the pill will kill the heartworms at all stages of development, the pill would be effective in killing larvae, nymphs or adults, and it takes four months for the larvae to reach the adult stage. Thus, there is no rationale to poisoning the dog's system on a monthly basis. Lastly, do not give the pill during the winter months since there are no mosquitoes around to pass on their infection, unless you live in a tropical environment.

Life Cycle of the Heartworm

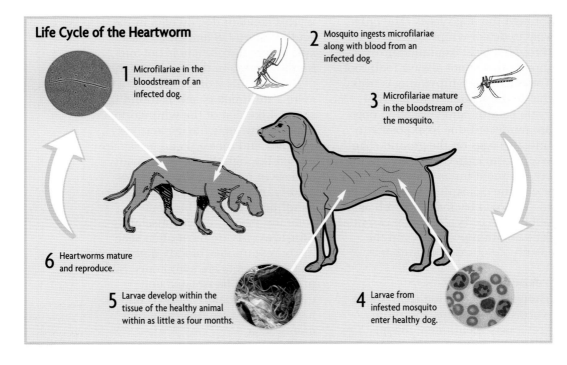

1 Microfilariae in the bloodstream of an infected dog.

2 Mosquito ingests microfilariae along with blood from an infected dog.

3 Microfilariae mature in the bloodstream of the mosquito.

6 Heartworms mature and reproduce.

5 Larvae develop within the tissue of the healthy animal within as little as four months.

4 Larvae from infested mosquito enter healthy dog.

HEARTWORMS

Heartworms are thin, extended worms up to 12 inches long, which live in a dog's heart and the major blood vessels surrounding it. Dogs may have up to 200 worms. Symptoms may be loss of energy, loss of appetite, coughing, the development of a pot belly and anemia.

Heartworms are transmitted by mosquitoes. The mosquito drinks the blood of an infected dog and takes in larvae with the blood. The larvae, called microfilariae, develop within the body of the mosquito and are passed on to the next dog bitten after the larvae mature. It takes two to three weeks for the larvae to develop to the infective stage within the body of the mosquito. Dogs are usually treated at about six weeks of age and maintained on a prophylactic dose given monthly.

Blood testing for heartworms is not necessarily indicative of how seriously your dog is infected. Although this is a dangerous disease, it is not easy for a dog to be infected. Discuss the various preventatives with your vet, as there are many different types now available. Together you can decide on a safe course of prevention for your dog.

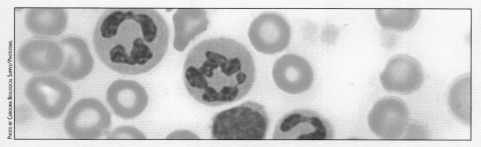

Magnified heart-worm larvae, *Diro-filaria immitis*.

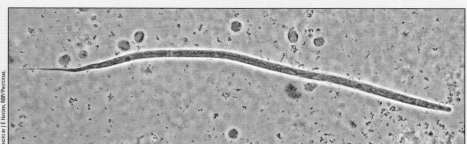

Heartworm, *Diro-filaria immitis*.

The heart of a dog infected with canine heart-worm, *Dirofilaria immitis*.

12 WAYS TO PREVENT BLOAT

Gastric torsion or bloat is a preventable killer of dogs. We know that bloat affects more large dogs and deep-chested dogs than any other dogs. Bloat can be defined as the rapid accumulation of air in the stomach, causing it to twist or flip over, thereby blocking the entrance and exit. A dog suffering from bloat experiences acute pain and is unable to release the gas. Shock and eventual dealth can result quickly. Here are some excellent recommendations to prevent this life-threatening condition.

- Do not provide water at mealtimes, especially for dogs that commonly drink large amounts of water
- Keep your dog at his proper weight. Avoid overfeeding.
- Limit exercise for at least one hour before and after mealtime.
- Avoid stressful or vigorous exercise altogether.
- Provide antacids for any dog with audible stomach motions (borborygmus) or flatulence.
- Feed two or three smaller meals instead of one large meal per day.
- Serve your dog's food and water on a bowl stand so that he does not have to crane his neck to eat and drink.
- Be certain that mealtime is a non-stressful time. Feed the dog alone, where he is not competing with a canine or feline housemate for his bowl. Feeding the dog in his crate is an excellent solution.
- For the big gulper, place large toys in the dog's bowl so that he cannot gulp his portions. Never allow him to gulp water.
- Discuss bloat prevention and preventative surgical methods with your veterinarian.
- If changing your dog's diet, do so gradually.
- Recognize the symptoms of bloat, as time is of the essence. Symptoms include pacing, whining, retching (with no result), groaning, obvious discomfort.

FATTY RISKS

Any dog of any breed can suffer from obesity. Studies show that nearly 30% of our dogs are overweight, primarily from high caloric intake and low energy expenditure. The hound and gundog breeds are the most likely affected, and females are at a greater risk of obesity than males. Pet dogs that are neutered are twice as prone to obesity as intact, whole dogs, although this is easily avoided with proper feeding and exercise.

CDS: COGNITIVE DYSFUNCTION SYNDROME
"Old-Dog Syndrome"

There are many ways for you to evaluate old-dog syndrome. Veterinarians have defined CDS (cognitive dysfunction syndrome) as the gradual deterioration of cognitive abilities. These are indicated by changes in the dog's behavior. When a dog changes his routine response, and maladies have been eliminated as the cause of these behavioral changes, then CDS is the usual diagnosis.

More than half the dogs over eight years old suffer from some form of CDS. The older the dog, the more chance he has of suffering from CDS. In humans, doctors often dismiss the CDS behavioral changes as part of "winding down."

There are four major signs of CDS: frequent potty accidents inside the home, sleeping much more or much less than normal, acting confused and failing to respond to social stimuli.

SYMPTOMS OF CDS

FREQUENT POTTY ACCIDENTS
- *Urinates in the house.*
- *Defecates in the house.*
- *Doesn't signal that he wants to go out.*

SLEEP PATTERNS
- *Awakens more slowly.*
- *Sleeps more than normal during the day.*
- *Sleeps less during the night.*

CONFUSION
- *Goes outside and just stands there.*
- *Appears confused with a faraway look in his eyes.*
- *Hides more often.*
- *Doesn't recognize friends.*
- *Doesn't come when called.*
- *Walks around listlessly and without a destination.*

FAILURE TO RESPOND TO SOCIAL STIMULI
- *Comes to people less frequently, whether called or not.*
- *Doesn't tolerate petting for more than a short time.*
- *Doesn't come to the door when you return home.*

YOUR SENIOR

GREYHOUND

As your Greyhound becomes gray and the wind diminishes beneath his windhound sails, it's time to consider that even the majestic Greyhound is a mortal creature. Owners never want to face the reality of their dogs' growing old and dying, but, unfortunately, this is the sad reality of dog ownership. Perhaps this is the price we pay for unconditional love from our canine best friends.

Puppies and adults love to play with their masters, thoroughly enjoying a chance to stretch their long legs in the park, on a jog or just in the backyard. As your Greyhound nears the ten-year mark, you will notice that he has begun to slow down considerably. If, on the other hand, you and your Greyhound have not led a very active lifestyle, the shift to "couch potato" may not be so obvious.

If people live to be 100 years old, dogs live to be 20 years old. While this may sound like a good rule of thumb, it is very inaccurate. When trying to compare dog years to human years, you cannot make a generalization about all dogs. You can make the generalization that 13 or 14 years is a good lifespan for a Greyhound, which is quite good compared to many other pure-bred dogs that may only live to 8 or 9 years of age. Dogs are generally considered mature within three years, but they can reproduce even earlier. So the first three years of a dog's life are like seven times that of comparable humans. That means a 3-year-old dog is like a 21-year-old human. As the curve of comparison shows, there is no hard and fast rule for comparing dog and human ages. The comparison is made even more difficult, for not all humans age at the same rate.

GETTING OLD

The bottom line is simply that a dog is getting old when you think he is getting old because he slows down in his general activities, including walking, running, eating, jumping and retrieving. On the other hand, certain activities increase, like more sleeping, more barking and more repetition of habits like going to the door when you put your coat on without being called.

WHAT TO LOOK FOR IN SENIORS

Most veterinarians and behaviorists use the seven-year mark as the time to consider a dog a senior. The term *senior* does not imply that the dog is geriatric and has begun to fail in mind and body. Aging is essentially a slowing process. Humans readily admit that they feel a difference in their activity level from age 20 to 30, and then from 30 to 40, etc. By treating the seven-year-old dog as a senior, owners are able to implement certain therapeutic and preventative medical strategies with the help of their veterinari-

HORMONAL PROBLEMS

Although graying is normal and expected in older dogs, a flaky coat or loss of hair is not. Such coat problems may point to a hormonal problem. Hypothyroidism, in which the thyroid gland fails to produce the normal amount of hormones, is one such problem. Your veterinarian can treat hypothyroidism with an oral supplement. The condition is more common in certain breeds, so discuss its likelihood in your dog with your breeder and vet.

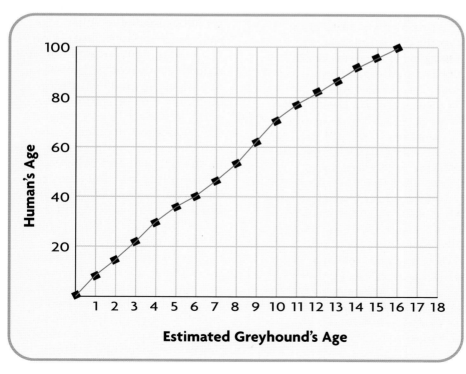

Estimated Greyhound's Age

ans. A senior-care program should include at least two veterinary visits per year and screening sessions to determine the dog's health status, as well as nutritional counseling. Veterinarians determine the senior dog's health status through a blood smear for a complete blood count, serum chemistry profile with electrolytes, urinalysis, blood pressure check, electrocardiogram, ocular tonometry (pressure on the eyeball) and dental prophylaxis.

NOTICING THE SYMPTOMS

The symptoms listed below are symptoms that gradually appear and become more noticeable. They are not life-threatening; however, the symptoms below are to be taken very seriously and warrant a discussion with your veterinarian:
- Your dog cries and whimpers when he moves, and he stops running completely.
- Convulsions start or become more serious and frequent. The usual convulsion (spasm) is when the dog stiffens and starts to tremble, being unable or unwilling to move. The seizure usually lasts for 5 to 30 minutes.
- Your dog drinks more water and urinates more frequently. Wetting and bowel accidents take place indoors without warning.
- Vomiting becomes more and more frequent.

Such an extensive program for senior dogs is well advised before owners start to see the obvious physical signs of aging, such as slower and inhibited movement, graying, increased sleep/nap periods and disinterest in play and other activity. This preventative program promises a longer, healthier life for the aging dog. Among the physical problems common in aging dogs are the loss of sight and hearing, arthritis, kidney and liver failure, diabetes mellitus, heart disease and Cushing's disease (a hormonal disease).

In addition to the physical manifestations discussed, there are some behavioral changes and problems related to aging dogs. Dogs suffering from hearing or vision loss, dental discomfort or arthritis can become aggressive. Likewise, the near-deaf and/or blind dog may be startled more easily and react in an unexpectedly aggressive manner. Seniors suffering from senility can become more impatient and irritable. Housesoiling accidents are associated with loss of mobility, kidney problems and loss of sphincter control as well as plaque accumulation, physiological brain changes and reactions to medications. Older dogs, just like young puppies, can suffer from separation anxiety, which can lead to excessive barking, whining, housesoiling and destructive behavior. Seniors may become fearful of everyday sounds, such as vacuum cleaners, heaters, thunder and passing traffic. Some dogs have difficulty sleeping, due to discomfort, the need for frequent potty visits and the like.

Owners should avoid spoiling the older dog with too many treats. Obesity is a common problem in older dogs and subtracts years from their lives. Keep the senior dog as trim as possible since excess weight puts additional stress on the body's vital organs. Some breeders recommend supplementing the diet with foods high in fiber and lower in calories. Adding fresh vegetables and marrow broth to the senior's diet makes a tasty, low-calorie, low-fat supplement. Vets also offer specialty diets for senior dogs that are worth exploring.

Your dog, as he nears his

twilight years, needs his owner's patience and good care more than ever. Never punish an older dog for an accident or abnormal behavior. For all the years of love, protection and companionship that your dog has provided, he deserves special attention and courtesies. The older dog may need to relieve himself at 3 a.m. because he can no longer hold it for eight hours. Older dogs may not be able to remain crated for more than two or three hours. It may be time to give up a sofa or chair to your old friend. Although he may not seem as enthusiastic about your attention and petting, he does appreciate the considerations you offer as he gets older.

Your Greyhound does not understand why his world is slowing down. Owners must make their dogs' transition into their golden years as pleasant and rewarding as possible.

Older dogs, besides getting gray on their face and paws, slow down considerably and rest frequently.

CONSISTENCY COUNTS

Puppies and older dogs are very similar in their need for consistency in their lives. Older pets may experience hearing and vision loss, or may just be more easily confused by changes in their homes. Try to keep things consistent for the senior dog. For example, doors that are always open or closed should remain so. Most importantly, don't dismiss a pet just because he's getting old; most senior dogs remain active and important parts of their owners' lives.

WHAT TO DO
WHEN THE TIME COMES

You are never fully prepared to make a rational decision about putting your dog to sleep. It is very obvious that you love your Greyhound or you would not be reading this book. Putting a loved dog to sleep is extremely difficult. It is a decision that must be made with your veterinarian. You are usually forced to make the decision when your dog experiences one or more life-threatening symptoms, requiring you to seek veterinary help.

If the prognosis of the malady indicates the end is near and your beloved pet will only suffer more and experience no enjoyment for the balance of his life, then euthanasia is the right choice.

What Is Euthanasia?

Euthanasia derives from the Greek, meaning *good death*. In other words, it means the planned, painless killing of a dog suffering from a painful, incurable condition, or who is so aged that he cannot walk, see, eat or control his excretory functions.

Euthanasia is usually accomplished by injection with an overdose of an anesthesia or barbiturate.

> ### EUTHANASIA SERVICES
> Euthanasia must be done by a licensed vet, who may be considerate enough to come to your home. There also may be societies for the prevention of cruelty to animals in your area. They often offer this service upon a vet's recommendation.

Aside from the prick of the needle, the experience is usually painless.

Making the Decision

The decision to euthanize your dog is never easy. The days during which the dog becomes ill and the end occurs can be unusually stressful for you. If this is your first experience with the death of a loved one, you may need the comfort dictated by your religious beliefs. If you are the head of the family and have children, you should have involved them in the decision of putting your Greyhound to sleep. Usually your dog can be maintained on drugs for a few days in the vet's clinic in order to give you ample time to make a decision. During this time, talking with members of your family or even people who have lived through this same experience can ease the burden of your inevitable decision.

The Final Resting Place

Dogs can have some of the same privileges as humans. They can possibly be buried in a pet cemetery, which is generally expensive. If your dog has died at home, he can be buried in your yard in a place suitably marked with a special stone or a newly planted tree or bush. Alternatively, dogs can be cremated individually, with the ashes returned to their owners. Some people prefer to leave their dogs at the veterinarians clinic.

All of these options should be

discussed frankly and openly with your veterinarian. Do not be afraid to ask financial questions. Cremations can be individual, but a less expensive option is mass cremation, although of course the ashes of individual dogs cannot then be returned. Vets can usually arrange cremation services or help you locate a suitable pet cemetery if you choose one of these options.

GETTING ANOTHER DOG?

The grief of losing your beloved dog will be as lasting as the grief of losing a human friend or relative. In most cases, if your dog died of old age (if there is such a thing), he had slowed down considerably. Do you want to rescue a Greyhound from an adoption agency? This, of course, is an excellent option and may well save the life of a wonderful member of this noble breed.

The decision is, of course, your own. Do you want another Greyhound or perhaps a different breed so as to avoid comparison with your beloved friend? Most people usually choose the same breed because they know and love the characteristics of that breed. Once you know the charms of the Greyhound, you will be hooked for life.

The greatest service we can offer our departed Greyhound is to open your heart and home to another member of his noble breed. Whether you decide to purchase a new Greyhound puppy or to adopt an ex-racer, you are

Many pet cemeteries have facilities for storing a dog's ashes.

paying your dog homage. Surely, the option of adopting an adult Greyhound from a rescue agency is most rewarding, as you may indeed be saving the life of a member of the Greyhound breed.

Some owners, however, may choose not to purchase or adopt a Greyhound, but instead to "downsize" to a different, smaller sight hound. Older owners often find that the Greyhound is too much to handle and therefore choose a Whippet, Basenji or Italian Greyhound. Regardless of which breed of dog you choose, once you are ready to take on a new canine companion, you will be ever so glad that you did. A home without a Greyhound is no home at all!

Often a beloved deceased Greyhound is laid to rest in the owner's yard in a suitably marked gravesite.

SHOWING YOUR
GREYHOUND

CONFORMATION BASICS

If you purchased a Greyhound puppy with definite plans to show him, then you will have informed the breeder of your intentions. Not every Greyhound puppy will grow up to be a show-dog candidate, so the breeder's input and advice are critical to your potential success in conformation showing.

To the novice, exhibiting a Greyhound in the show ring may look easy, but it takes a lot of hard work and devotion to do top winning at a show such as the prestigious Westminster Kennel Club, Crufts or World Dog Show, not to mention a little luck, too!

The first concept that the canine novice learns when watching a dog show is that each dog first competes against members of his own breed. Once the judge has selected the best member of each breed (Best of Breed), provided that the show is judged on a Group system, that chosen dog will compete with other dogs in his group. Finally, the dogs chosen first in each group will compete for Best in Show.

The second concept that you must understand is that the dogs are not actually compared against one another. The judge compares each dog against his breed's standard. While some early breed standards were indeed based on specific dogs that were famous or popular, many dedicated enthusiasts say that a perfect specimen, as described in the standard, has never walked into a show ring, has never been bred and, to the woe of dog breeders around the globe, does not exist. Breeders attempt to get as close to this ideal as possible with every litter, but theoretically the "perfect" dog is so elusive that it is impossible.

If you are interested in exploring the world of dog showing, your best bet is to join your local breed club or the national

AKC GROUPS

For showing purposes, the American Kennel Club divides its recognized breeds into seven groups: Hounds, Sporting Dogs, Working Dogs, Terriers, Toys, Non-Sporting Dogs and Herding Dogs.

parent club, which is the Greyhound Club of America (GCA). The GCA and local clubs host specialty shows in which only Greyhounds can compete. The National Specialty is held by the GCA annually in a different location each year. Specialties are exciting for fanciers and fans alike, as they include not only conformation classes but also obedience trials, lure coursing and more! Clubs also send out newsletters, and some organize training days and seminars in order that people may learn more about their chosen breed. To find out more about entering shows, contact the American Kennel Club, which furnishes the rules and regulations for all of these events plus general dog registration and other basic requirements of dog ownership.

If your Greyhound is of age and registered, you can enter him in a dog show where the breed is offered classes. Only unaltered dogs can be entered in a dog show, so if you have spayed or neutered your Greyhound, you cannot compete in conformation shows. The reason for this is simple. Dog shows are the main forum to prove which representatives of a breed are worthy of being bred. Only dogs that have proven themselves in the show ring by attaining a Champion title—the recognized "seal of approval" for excellence

A matched pair (or brace) of Greyhounds being displayed at a dog show. Although once known solely as racers, the number of Greyhounds in the conformation ring is increasing all over the world.

BECOMING A CHAMPION

An official AKC champion of record requires that a dog accumulate 15 points under three different judges, including two "majors" under different judges. Points are awarded based on the number of dogs entered into competition, varying from breed to breed and place to place. A win of three, four or five points is considered a "major." The AKC annually assigns a schedule of points to adjust to the variations that accompany a breed's popularity and the population of a given area.

in pure-bred dogs—should be bred. Altered dogs, however, can participate in other events such as obedience trials and the Canine Good Citizen® program, although not in lure coursing.

Before you actually step into the ring, you would be well advised to sit back and observe the judge's ring procedure. If it is your first time in the ring, do not be over-anxious and run to the front of the line. It is much better to stand back and study how the exhibitor in front of you is performing. The judge asks each

> ## SHOW-RING ETIQUETTE
>
> Just as with anything else, there is a certain etiquette to the show ring that can only be learned through experience. Showing your dog can be quite intimidating to you as a novice when it seems as if everyone else knows what he is doing. You can familiarize yourself with ring procedure beforehand by taking showing classes to prepare you and your dog for conformation showing and by talking with experienced handlers. When you are in the ring, it is very important to pay attention and listen to the instructions you are given by the judge about where to move your dog. Remember, even the most skilled handlers had to start somewhere. Keep it up and you too will become a proficient handler as you gain practice and experience.

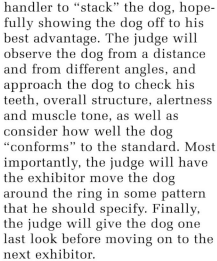

handler to "stack" the dog, hopefully showing the dog off to his best advantage. The judge will observe the dog from a distance and from different angles, and approach the dog to check his teeth, overall structure, alertness and muscle tone, as well as consider how well the dog "conforms" to the standard. Most importantly, the judge will have the exhibitor move the dog around the ring in some pattern that he should specify. Finally, the judge will give the dog one last look before moving on to the next exhibitor.

If you are not in the top four in your class at your first show, do not be discouraged. Be patient and consistent, and you may eventually find yourself in a winning line-up. Remember that the winners were once in your shoes and have devoted many hours and much money to earn the placement. If you find that your dog is losing every time and never getting a nod, it may be time to consider a different dog sport or to just enjoy your Greyhound as a pet.

OBEDIENCE TRIALS

Obedience trials in the US trace back to the early 1930s when organized obedience training was developed to demonstrate how well dog and owner could work together. The pioneer of obedience trials is Mrs. Helen White-

This Greyhound is being gaited before the judges to have his movement appraised. What a graceful walk!

house Walker, a Standard Poodle fancier, who designed a series of exercises after the Associated, Sheep, Police, Army Dog Society of Great Britain. Since the days of Mrs. Walker, obedience trials have grown by leaps and bounds, and today there are over 2,000 trials held in the US every year, with more than 100,000 dogs competing. Any AKC-registered dog can enter an obedience trial, regardless of conformational disqualifications or neutering.

Obedience trials are divided into three levels of progressive difficulty. At the first level, the Novice, dogs compete for the title Companion Dog (CD); at the intermediate level, the Open, dogs compete for the title

FIVE CLASSES AT SHOWS

At most AKC all-breed shows, there are five regular classes offered: Puppy, Novice, Bred-by-Exhibitor, American-bred and Open. The Puppy Class is usually divided as 6 to 9 months of age and 9 to 12 months of age. When deciding in which class to enter your dog, male or female, you must carefully check the show schedule to make sure that you have selected the right class. Depending on the age of the dog, previous first-place wins and the sex of the dog, you must make the best choice. It is possible to enter a one-year-old dog who has not won sufficient first places in any of the non-Puppy Classes, though the competition is more intense the further you progress from the Puppy Class.

Companion Dog Excellent (CDX); and at the advanced level, the Utility, dogs compete for the title Utility Dog (UD). Classes are subdivided into "A" (for beginners) and "B" (for more experienced handlers). A perfect score at any level is 200, and a dog must score 170 or better to earn a "leg," of which three are needed to earn the title. To earn points, the dog must score more than 50% of the available points in each exercise; the possible points range from 20 to 40.

Each level consists of a different set of exercises. In the Novice level, the dog must heel on- and off-lead, come, long sit, long down and stand for examination. These skills are the basic ones required for a well-behaved "Companion Dog." The Open level requires that the dog perform the same exercises as in the Novice but without a leash for extended lengths of time, as well as retrieve a dumbbell, broad jump and drop on recall. In the Utility level, dogs must perform ten difficult exercises, including scent discrimination, hand signals for basic commands, directed jump and directed retrieve.

Once a dog has earned the UD title, he can compete with other proven obedience dogs for the coveted title of Utility Dog Excellent (UDX), which requires that the dog win "legs" in ten shows. Utility Dogs who earn "legs" in Open B and Utility B earn points toward their Obedience Trial Champion title. In 1977, the title Obedience Trial Champion (OTCh.) was established by the AKC. To become an OTCh., a dog needs to earn 100 points, which requires three first places in Open B and Utility under three different judges.

AGILITY TRIALS

Having had its origins in the UK back in 1977, AKC agility had its official beginning in the US in August 1994, when the first licensed agility trials were held. The AKC allows all registered breeds to participate, providing the dog is 12 months of age or older. Agility is designed so that the handler demonstrates how

PRACTICE AT HOME

If you have decided to show your dog, you must train him to gait around the ring by your side at the correct pace and pattern, and to tolerate being handled and examined by the judge. Most breeds require complete dentition, all breeds require a particular bite (scissors, level or undershot) and all males must have two apparently normal testicles fully descended into the scrotum. Enlist family and friends to hold mock trials in your yard to prepare your future champion!

try. Both the USDAA and the AKC offer titles to winning dogs. Three titles are available through the USDAA: Agility Dog (AD), Advanced Agility Dog (AAD) and Master Agility Dog (MAD). The AKC offers Novice Agility (NA), Open Agility (OA), Agility Excellent (AX) and Master Agility Excellent (MX). Beyond these four AKC titles, dogs can win additional ones in "jumper" classes, Jumpers with Weave Novice (NAJ), Open (OAJ) and Excellent (MXJ), which lead to the ultimate title(s): MACH, Master Agility Champion. Dogs can continue to add number

Hopes for a championship! It can take months, sometimes years, of training and practice for both dog and handler before that elusive championship title is earned.

well the dog can work at his side. The handler directs his dog over an obstacle course that includes jumps as well as tires, the dog walk, weave poles, pipe tunnels, collapsed tunnels, etc. While working his way through the course, the dog must keep one eye and ear on the handler and the rest of his body on the course. The handler gives verbal and hand signals to guide the dog through the course.

The first organization to promote agility trials in the US was the United States Dog Agility Association, Inc. (USDAA), which was established in 1986 and spawned numerous member clubs around the coun-

CLUB CONTACTS

You can get information about dog shows from the national kennel clubs:

American Kennel Club
5580 Centerview Dr., Raleigh, NC 27606-3390
www.akc.org

United Kennel Club
100 E. Kilgore Road, Kalamazoo, MI 49002
www.ukcdogs.com

Canadian Kennel Club
89 Skyway Ave., Suite 100, Etobicoke,
Ontario M9W 6R4, Canada
www.ckc.ca

The Kennel Club
1-5 Clarges St., Piccadilly,
London W1Y 8AB, UK
www.the-kennel-club.org.uk

At a major international dog show in Holland, the Greyhound took Hound Group 2.

famous races beginning in England, such as the Waterloo Cup for Greyhounds that dates back to 1836. The sport of lure coursing in the US is a much more recent phenomenon, having begun in the 1970s by gaze-hound fancier Lyle Gillette and some hunting enthusiasts. Since hunting in open fields is fairly dangerous, and not common or legal in many places, the need for a simulated event arose and lure coursing was the answer. Lure coursing allows owners to give their dogs a forum to test their field abilities without actually working on an open field in pursuit of jackrabbits or the like. Usually these events use plastic bags or white fur dummies, which give the dog the impression of game escaping through the course. Dogs are scored based on how well they follow the lure, their enthusiasm for the chase and their agility, speed and endurance.

designations to the MACH titles, indicating how many times the dog has met the MACH requirements, such as MACH1, MACH2 and so forth.

Agility is great fun for dog and owner with many rewards for everyone involved. Interested owners should join a training club that has obstacles and experienced agility handlers who can introduce you and your dog to the "ropes" (and tires, tunnels and more).

LURE COURSING
Sight-hound owners are fortunate to have the chance to try their dogs at lure coursing! Coursing events have been popular around the world, with many

The American Kennel Club sanctions lure coursing for Greyhounds and other sight-hound breeds and these are sponsored by member clubs. Dogs are required to be one year of age or older in order to participate, and unlike obedience trials, dogs must not have any disqualifying fault, which includes spaying and neutering. The AKC offers three suffix titles to winning dogs: Junior Courser (JC), Senior

Courser (SC) and Master Courser (MC); the most prestigious AKC title is the prefix Field Champion (FC). There are also non-competitive events sponsored by affiliated clubs, fun-filled meets that are ideal for the novice courser.

The AKC National Lure Coursing Championship is the annual event where the best of the best sight hounds from around the country come together to compete. This two-day event usually attracts over 100 titled sight hounds, including many Dual Champions and Field Champions. The qualifications to participate are steep and include a Best of Breed or three-point "major" win at a regional or championship event. The event moves to different venues each year but always proves to

Pure speed, form and an extended body that is unique in dogdom and never fails to impress.

be the most exciting coursing event of the year.

Field trials also are held every weekend by organizations like the American Sighthound Field Association (ASFA), which has over 100 member clubs. Newcomers are encouraged to visit the club's website (www.asfa.org) to locate local clubs and to contact one of the regional directors, who can assist interested parties in getting started in lure coursing.

Sight hounds at ASFA coursing events will run the designated course twice, with the scores from each run combined to determine a final score. Based on how many dogs compete and where the dog completes the course, the dog is awarded placements and points. The ASFA awards a Field Champion title to any dog that earns 100 points and two first places (or two second places and one first place). Beyond this title, a dog can earn a Lure Courser of Merit title for further coursing accomplishments.

Your Greyhound must stand still while the judge evaluates overall conformation, which includes an inspection of musculature, coat, overall structure and, in a male, fully descended testicles.

BEHAVIOR OF YOUR
GREYHOUND

As a Greyhound owner, you have selected your dog so that you and your loved ones can have a companion, a running mate, a friend and a four-legged family member. You invest time, money and effort to care for and train the family's new charge. Of course, this chosen canine behaves perfectly! Well, perfectly like a *dog*.

THINK LIKE A DOG
Dogs do not think like humans, nor do humans think like dogs, though we try. Unfortunately, a dog is incapable of figuring out how humans think, so the respon-

sibility falls on the owner to adopt a good canine mindset. Dogs cannot rationalize, and they only exist in the present moment. Many a dog owner makes the mistake in training of thinking that he can reprimand his dog for something the dog did a while ago. Basically, you cannot even reprimand a dog for something he did 20 seconds ago! Either catch him in the act or forget it! It is a waste of your and your dog's time—in his mind, you are reprimanding him for whatever he is doing at that moment.

The following behavioral problems represent some which owners most commonly encounter. Every dog is unique and every situation is unique. No author could purport for you to solve your Greyhound's problem simply by reading a chapter in a breed book. Here we outline some basic "dogspeak" so that owners' chances of solving behavioral problems are increased. Discuss bad habits with your veterinarian and he can recommend a behavioral specialist to consult in appropriate cases. Since behav-

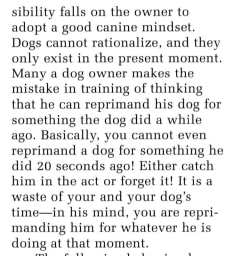

PROFESSIONAL TRAINING
If your dog barks menacingly or growls at strangers, or if he growls at anyone who comes near him while he is eating, playing with a toy or taking a rest in his favorite spot, he needs proper professional training because sooner or later this behavior can result in someone being bitten. Greyhounds can be particular about their "personal space," but should never be aggressive.

ioral abnormalities are the leading reason for owners' abandoning their pets, we hope that you will make a valiant effort to solve your Greyhound's problem. Patience and understanding are virtues that must dwell in every pet-loving household.

AGGRESSION

Aggression can be a very big problem in dogs and, when not controlled, always becomes dangerous. An aggressive dog, no matter the size, may lunge at, bite or even attack a person or another dog. Aggressive behavior is not to be tolerated. It is more than just inappropriate behavior; it is not safe. It is painful for a family to watch their dog become unpredictable in his behavior to the point where they are afraid of him. While not all aggressive behavior is dangerous, things like growling, baring teeth, etc., can be frightening. It is important to ascertain why the dog is acting in this manner. Aggression is a display of dominance, and the dog should not have the dominant role in his pack, which is, in this case, your family.

It is important not to challenge an aggressive dog as this could provoke an attack. Observe your Greyhound's body language. Does he make direct eye contact and stare? Does he try to make himself as large as

DOGS HAVE FEELINGS, TOO
You probably don't realize how much your dog notices the presence of a new person in your home as well as the loss of a familiar face. If someone new has moved in with you, your pet will need help adjusting. Have the person feed your dog or accompany the two of you on a walk. Also, make sure your roommate is aware of the rules and routines you have already set for your dog.

If you have just lost a longtime companion, there is a chance you could end up with a case of "leave me, leave my dog." Dogs experience separation anxiety and depression, so watch for any changes in sleeping and eating habits and try to lavish a little extra love on your dog. It might make you feel better, too.

possible: ears pricked, chest out, tail erect? Height and size signify authority in a dog pack—being taller or "above" another dog literally means that he is "above" in the social status. These body signals tell you that your Greyhound thinks he is in charge, a problem that needs to be addressed. An aggressive dog is unpredictable: you never know when he is going to strike and what he is going to do. You cannot understand why a dog that is playful and loving one minute is growling and snapping the next.

Greyhounds are generally considered gregarious hounds, accustomed to the company of other dogs.

The best solution is to consult a behavioral specialist, one who has experience with the Greyhound if possible. Together, perhaps you can pinpoint the cause of your dog's aggression and do something about it. An aggressive dog cannot be trusted, and a dog that cannot be trusted is not safe to have as a family pet. If, very unusually, you find that your pet has become untrustworthy and you feel it necessary to seek a new home with a more suitable family and environment, explain fully to the new owners all your reasons for re-homing the dog to be fair to all concerned.

AGGRESSION TOWARD OTHER DOGS

A dog's aggressive behavior toward another dog sometimes stems from insufficient exposure to other dogs at an early age. If other dogs make your Greyhound nervous and agitated, he will lash out as a defensive mechanism, though this behavior is thankfully uncommon in the breed. A dog who has not received sufficient exposure to other canines tends to believe that he is the only dog on the planet. The animal becomes so dominant that he does not even show signs that he is fearful or threatened. Without growling or any other physical signal as a warning, he will lunge at and bite the other dog.

A way to correct this is to let your Greyhound approach another dog when walking on lead. Watch very closely and, at the very first sign of aggression, correct your Greyhound and pull him away. Scold him for any sign of discomfort, and then praise him when he ignores or tolerates the other dog. Keep this up until he stops the aggressive behavior, learns to ignore the other dog or accepts other dogs. Praise him lavishly for this correct behavior.

SEXUAL BEHAVIOR

Dogs exhibit certain sexual behaviors that may have influenced your choice of male or female when you first purchased your Greyhound. To a certain extent, spaying/neutering will eliminate these behaviors, but if you are purchasing a dog that you wish to breed, you should be aware of what you will have to deal with throughout the dog's life.

Female dogs usually have two estruses per year with each season lasting about three weeks. These are the only times in which a female dog will mate, and she usually will not allow this until the second week of the cycle, but this does vary from bitch to bitch. If not bred during the heat cycle, it is not uncommon for a bitch to experience a false pregnancy, in which her mammary glands swell and she exhibits maternal tendencies toward toys or other objects.

Mounting is a fairly common behavior, and owners must recognize that mounting is not merely a sexual expression but also one of dominance, seen in males and females alike. Be consistent and persistent and you will find that you can "move mounters."

CHEWING

The national canine pastime is chewing! Every dog loves to sink his "canines" into a tasty bone, or whatever happens to be available for him to chew on. Dogs need to chew, to massage their gums, to make their new teeth feel better and to exercise their jaws. This is a natural behavior deeply imbedded in all things canine. Your role as owner is not to stop the dog's chewing, but to redirect it to positive, chew-worthy objects. Be an informed owner and purchase proper chew toys like strong nylon bones that will not splinter. Be sure that the devices are safe and durable, since your dog's safety is at risk. Again, the owner is responsible for ensuring a dog-proof environment.

The best answer is prevention: that is, put your shoes, handbags and other tasty objects in their proper places (out of the reach of the growing canine mouth). Direct your puppy to his

---

THE MIGHTY MALE

Males, whether castrated or not, will mount almost anything: a pillow, your leg or, much to your dismay, even your neighbor's leg. As with other types of inappropriate behavior, the dog must be corrected while in the act, which for once is not difficult. Often he will not let go! While a puppy is experimenting with his very first urges, his owners feel he needs to "sow his oats" and allow the pup to mount. As the pup grows into a full-size dog, with full-size urges, it becomes a nuisance and an embarrassment. Males always appear as if they are trying to "save the race," more determined and stronger than imaginable. While altering the dog at an appropriate age will limit the dog's desire, it usually does not remove it entirely.

toys whenever you see him tasting the furniture legs or the leg of your trousers. Make a loud noise to attract the pup's attention, and immediately escort him to his chew toy and engage him with the toy for at least four minutes, praising and encouraging him all the while.

Some trainers recommend deterrents, such as hot pepper or another bitter spice or a product designed for this purpose, to discourage the dog from chewing unwanted objects. Test these products with to see how they work with your own dog before investing in large quantities.

JUMPING UP

Jumping up is a dog's friendly way of saying hello! Some dog owners do not mind when their dog jumps up, which is fine for them. The problem arises when guests come to the house and the dog greets them in the same manner—whether they like it or not! However friendly the greeting may be, the chances are that your visitors will not appreciate your dog's enthusiasm. The dog will not be able to distinguish upon whom he can jump and whom he cannot. Therefore, it is probably best to discourage this behavior entirely, especially in a breed as tall and long-legged as the Greyhound.

Pick a command such as "Off" (avoid using "Down" since you will use that for the dog to lie down) and tell him "Off" when he jumps up. Place him on

Crates not only assist the owner in house-training but also give the owner a means to confine his Greyhound safely anytime the need arises.

the ground on all fours and have him sit, praising him the whole time. Always lavish him with praise and petting when he is in the sit position. That way you can instill polite manners while still giving him a warm affectionate greeting, because you are as excited to see him as he is to see you!

BARKING

Dogs cannot talk—oh, what they would say if they could! Instead, barking is a dog's way of "talking." It can be somewhat frustrating because it is not always easy to tell what a dog means by his bark—is he excited, happy, frightened or angry? Whatever it is that the dog is trying to say, he should not be punished for barking. It is only when the barking becomes excessive, and when the excessive barking becomes a bad habit, that the behavior needs to be modified.

Excessive habitual barking, however, is a problem that should be corrected early on. As your Greyhound grows up, you will be able to tell when his barking is purposeful and when it is for no reason. You will become able to distinguish your dog's different barks and their meanings. For example, the bark when someone comes to the door will be different from the bark when he is excited to see you. It is similar to a person's tone of voice, except

that the dog has to rely totally on tone of voice because he does not have the benefit of using words. An incessant barker will be evident at an early age.

There are some things that encourage a dog to bark. For example, if your dog barks nonstop for a few minutes and you give him a treat to quiet him, he believes that you are rewarding him for barking. He will associate barking with getting a treat, and will keep doing it until he is rewarded. If you give him a "Quiet" command and reward him when he's stopped barking, he will understand that being quiet is what you want him to do.

FOOD STEALING

Is your dog devising ways of stealing food from your coffee table and countertops? If so, you must answer the following questions: Is your Greyhound hungry, or is he "constantly famished" like many dogs seem to be? Face it, some dogs are more food-motivated than others. Some dogs are totally obsessed by the smell of food and can only think of their next meal. Food stealing is terrific fun and always yields a great reward—*food*, glorious food. Greyhounds are talented thieves, and their height makes many things accessible.

The owner's goal, therefore, is to be sensible about where

food is placed in the home, and to reprimand your dog whenever caught in the act of stealing. But remember, only reprimand the dog if you actually see him stealing, not later when the crime is discovered, for that will be of no use at all and will only serve to confuse.

BEGGING
Just like food stealing, begging is a favorite pastime of hungry puppies! It yields that same awesome result—*food!* Dogs quickly learn that their owners keep the "good food" for ourselves, and that we humans do not dine on kibble alone. Begging is a conditioned response related to a specific stimulus, time and place. The sounds of the kitchen, cans and bottles opening, crinkling bags, the smell of food in preparation, etc., will excite the dog and soon the paws are in the air!

Here is the solution to stop-

ping this behavior: Never give in to a beggar! You are rewarding the dog for sitting pretty, jumping up, whining and rubbing his nose into you by giving him food. By ignoring the dog, you will (eventually) force the behavior into extinction. Note that the behavior likely gets worse before it disappears, so be sure there are not any "softies" in the family who will give in to little "Oliver" every time he whimpers, "More, please."

SEPARATION ANXIETY
Your Greyhound may howl, whine or otherwise vocalize his displeasure at your leaving the house and his being left alone. This is a normal reaction, no different from the child who cries as his mother leaves him on the first day at school. However, separation anxiety is more serious and can lead to destructive behaviors. Constant attention can lead to separation anxiety in the first place. If you are endlessly fussing over your dog, he will come to expect this from you all of the time and it will be more traumatic for him when you are not there. Obviously, you enjoy spending time with your dog, and he thrives

on your love and attention. However, it should not become a dependent relationship where he is heartbroken without you.

One thing you can do to minimize separation anxiety is to make your entrances and exits as low-key as possible. Do not give your dog a long drawn-out goodbye, and do not lavish him with hugs and kisses when you return. This is giving in to the attention that he craves, and it will only make him miss it more when you are away. Another thing you can try is to give your dog a treat when you leave; this will not only keep him occupied and keep his mind off the fact that you have just left, but it will also help him associate your leaving with a pleasant experience.

You may have to accustom your dog to being left alone in intervals. Of course, when your Greyhound starts whimpering as you approach the door, your first instinct will be to run to him and comfort him, but do not do it! Eventually he will adjust and be just fine if you take it in small steps. His anxiety stems from being placed in an unfamiliar situation; by familiarizing him with being alone, he will learn that he is okay. That is not to say you should purposely leave your dog home alone, but the dog needs to know that, while he can depend on you for his care, you do not have to be by his side 24 hours a day.

When the dog is alone in the house, he should be confined to his designated dog-proof area of the house. This should be the area in which he sleeps and already feels comfortable so he will feel more at ease when he is alone.

Traffic markers are placed in the kennel areas so the male dogs can use them as "posts" on which they can lift their legs to urinate.

INDEX

My Greyhound

Dog's Name _____

Date _____ Photographer _____